The Nature of Being

By G.W. Pfister

@GWPfister
www.gwpfister.com

Published by
Gary W. Pfister
Barrington, IL
www.gwpfister.com

Library of Congress Cataloging-in-Publication Data
is available upon request.

ISBN: 978-0-692-88358-7

Printed in the United States of America

LOVE ALWAYS, ALWAYS LOVE

For Allie & Julia…One & All

Preface

This book was written over a two and a half year period, during a time of continuous acts of terror occurring throughout the world. I hope as you read this you now live in an era where fear is no longer the common thread we all share, and has since been replaced by love.

There is nothing more sacred than life. We have all been given a great gift to experience it and to know its love. We all have the inherent means to do the work, enjoy its fruits and appreciate all that it offers. How we choose to live our lives defines our story. It also helps define how others live their lives and thus, their actions have a similar bearing on yours.

It is our moral obligation to make choices that affect the good of all in a positive way. Nothing is achieved that has any lasting benefit when created contrary to our responsibility toward community and compassion.

Together, we have the ability to achieve many great things, to expand beyond our physical limitations, and realize our true potential. Each one of us has been given the necessary tools to create from love, as we are intended.

That is our Nature of Being!

Acknowledgements

This author would like to acknowledge all who have participated in the making of this book. To all the great teachers, past and present, who continue to shine the light of love. I have been greatly influenced by the likes of Les Brown, Dr. Wayne Dyer, Dan Millman, and Dr. Darren Weissman - all at pivotal moments in my life. Their inspiration has moved me profoundly, helping create the foundation of my expression.

I cannot identify any single person or piece of literature that first fueled my passion to this path of discovery. So much of what these teachers have shown me seems familiar, even as I was hearing it for the first time. Wayne Dyer often said that it was not he who writes. It was the hand of God writing through him, and he was but a vehicle for God's teachings. I believe that to be true, as God is guiding me this moment.

I want to thank the Foundation for Inner Peace and *A Course in Miracles* for inspiring my deeper spiritual understanding and allowing me to use excerpts in this book. *A Course in Miracles* is a game changer!

To my Mom and Dad, for making me possible, raising me the best you could, and inspiring me to seek knowledge, imagine greater, and to dream bigger. My mom was my first motivational speaker! Her dinnertime soapbox speeches were not lost on me. They were the spark that allowed me to think openly and envision what the mind is capable of.

To my family members and friends who supported me in this venture – Thank you. I especially want to thank Terry Pfister, for providing her professional writing skills and consultation.

To all the loves in my life who have allowed me to experience intimacy and companionship, furthering my understanding of how to treat people, helping me become the person I'm supposed to be - Love always. To Dorotka, an angel sent to me as a gift of God, just when I needed you most.

Finally, to my daughters Julia and Allison - You allow me to fully understand love. Nothing has changed my beliefs about what is important in life more than having your presence in mine. Thank you for teaching me and joining me for the ride.

And to you the reader, thank you for joining me as well!

Contents

The Nature of Being

A Gentle Guide to
Inspiring Greater Love

Introduction

Thoughts from My 23 Year-Old Self:

"I look around me and I see a world that's living, something independent from myself yet entirely codependent of all its parts, that which I am a part of. How significant am I to this whole? I look around and see the fibers beneath me. The Earth. The true substance from which we came. We are but passengers of life on this living wonder. Our home...at least for the time being.

It is easy to detach myself from the whole and say, "I am a man, and all this around me is mine to do as I wish. And, that it is." Yet, as a man, I only see what my eyes show me. I hear, smell and feel only what the limitations of my body allow, but there is so much more. Beneath my feet there is soil, and to me that's about all it is. Science has shown me that it is a compilation of decayed matter, gravel and air. Even I can see that if I look hard enough. But what science also tells me is something I cannot see. The complexity of it all. The molecules and atoms. The essence of what we and everything around us are made from.

We take for granted that the Earth is a pretty big place. We can all see that. What we cannot see is its immenseness, its enormity in relation to the atom. This is why it is so hard to comprehend mankind within the universe we inhabit. For man is but an atom in this universe, relatively speaking. So to ask what is man's purpose within the framework of the universe is a question that can only be rivaled in perplexity by asking what is my purpose amidst the millions and billions of stars in the universe. It's hard to believe, even impossible to think that the actions of my life will affect the whole network of things. Yet if an atom is nonexistent within a structure, the molecules would break down. I guess what I'm trying to say is simply; we are all, along with everything around us, the sum of the whole, raising the burning question of mankind...How do we all fit in?

I feel I was put here for a reason. What that is, I do not know. I only know the answer is not only within me but all around me."

I don't know why I kept the beat-up yellow legal pad that this was written on so many years ago. It's the ramblings of a young man trying to find his way. It sat in a box for years. I always knew it was there, and when my journey in life began to take a more spiritual path, I dug it up. After I read it, one of the first thoughts that came to my mind was - *Where did these ideas come from? What was the original source of my ideas?* Here I am now on a path of discovery, diving deep inside myself for answers. Then I find something I wrote in my early twenties, and I see how the ideas and consciousness of my modern self are so similar to it. All this time, I believed I was discovering this information for the first time, yet here it is, written by me so many years ago. It's as if this knowledge has been within me from the very beginning. I now believe that is exactly the case.

At an early age, I was in conflict with my Catholic upbringing and realized I no longer believed in the concept of original sin. It made no sense to me. Why would God in all his perfection create something imperfect, whose life's goal is to prove it is worthy of perfection? I insisted that there must be more to it than that. I was not a bad person. I was not a sinner. As long as I lived a life of goodness, Heaven would always be open to me.

I believe we are all born perfect. We all have the necessary information we need at birth to be as God intended us to be. It is life that teaches us to pick the apple from the tree. We choose whether we stray from our path.

I chose to strip away the notion that there is only one path to Heaven and live a life that has lead me through a maze of good and bad decisions, always taking the high road in the end. As I now dig deeper within myself, I realize that this is the foundation of my nature of being - my true nature. There are no accidents in life. We constantly make decisions that affect our course, and in my travels I have experienced enough of life to draw the following conclusions:

> Love is an absolute truth.
> Love connects all things.
> God is the source of all things.
> God is all things.
> All things are part of God.

Love is the connection; unspoken, unnamable, incalculable. It is the 'being' (verb) that transcends the mystical unknown world to the world of substance and reality. Reality - being a term to describe our human experience.

Life is a finite moment for what we define as ourselves. This is our physical existence. The person you are that allows you to separate from the source of all things is your ego-self. The person that exists as God intends is your natural-self. The ego-self creates the duality of your being.

It strives to show that you are separate and special from everything and everyone else. Meanwhile, your true nature (your natural-self) remains connected to all things. This duality of human beings creates the potential for choice, and the choices you make in life define the person you are and the experiences you have on your life's journey.

Only by being self-aware do you maintain your connection with source and your natural-self. Mindfulness, knowing the thoughts you keep, allows you to focus only on thoughts that originate from your loving source versus those of your ego-self. Maintaining this connection helps you make better decisions. Life then becomes less stressful and more joyful. As a result, the world becomes a better place, because joy is your greatest contribution to it.

Respect and reverence for all living things and an understanding of your connection to nature is your strongest defense against the ego's push for separation. Being mindful of your connection naturally raises your level of compassion, kindness, clarity and love. It frees you from judgments. It expands your awareness, giving you a better understanding of your purpose.

Love is the only guide you need through the decisions that define your journey in life. To better understand this, you will need to first take the journey within. The sooner you take this journey and discover your true-self, the less resistance you will experience along the way and the more fulfilling your life will be.

Life doesn't need to be hard or difficult, so don't make it so. The reason so many people never reach their true potential is because they place so much resistance in their own way. They exist outside of their true nature, allowing their ego to decide what is best for them. With so many people living individual, self-centered lives, we as a collective species will never reach our true potential in this current state of being. In order for there to be any actual change in the world, actual peace and prosperity, we all need to experience this inner journey and awaken to it.

If human beings lived in a flowing stream, we would quickly learn that it is easier to not fight the current. If we needed to move upstream, we would move closer to the banks where the water flows more slowly. So too, we must adjust our choices to achieve less resistance, to move more effortlessly within our lives and the world we live in.

Choice - is the life we lead, and we live by our choices. In all situations, there is only one right choice, and that is to choose love. We've not only been given the ability to comprehend it, but we also choose whether we want to be within its flow. It is the same as our choice to be happy. Happiness does not elude us. Love does not elude us. We make a choice to be happy and a choice to love.

Choices made collectively over time become our life lessons. Our choices define our existence in a Heaven and Hell here on Earth. And I want to emphasize this: Heaven and Hell are right here on Earth. Heaven will always open to us. Heaven is our infinite connection to God's source. It's where we return to once we leave this physical existence. We naturally live within its flow. However, we create our own personal Hell.

There is a clear path to Heaven through love, but we rarely follow it precisely. We meander, zigzagging our way, always being nudged closer to our true path through painful life lessons. When we are not acting within our true nature, we suffer. The pain we feel when we are not aligned with our source is God's way of gently nudging us back on our path. The further we move off course, the more we suffer and the greater pain we feel.

It has long been thought that competition within a species exists to ensure that the strongest survive, yet a human's ability to reason changes all of that. We have the ability to solve problems and ensure mutual survival. We have the means to feed the entire world and become the stewards of the environment. Yet we do not. Instead, we continue to fight and squabble over geopolitical gains and money. We use the precious resources of this planet as little more than a commodity. We have become too smart for our own good. After centuries of attempting to control nature, we have altered landscapes and interrupted natural processes for what we consider our divine right as God's pinnacle creation. That notion alone and the consequences of our actions have resulted in our greatest deviation from our true nature. We have separated ourselves from all other things. The ultimate victory for the ego is to think we are better or more special than anything else on this planet. Tell that to a virus.

We are a fragile species living on a fragile planet. Without appreciation and respect for all living things, and I include the Earth itself in this, we cannot sustain ourselves. The idea that we can alter and degrade our planet without suffering the consequences is foolhardy to say the least.

Far too many of us live our lives without feeling the earth beneath our feet. We live and work in high-rise buildings, walk on nothing but concrete, and then wonder why we feel so out of whack. Is it any coincidence we feel so good when we finally enjoy a brief vacation and sink our feet in the sand? It's only then that we are once again feeling connected to the land.

To feel this connection, it is not only important to connect on a physical level, but on a mental and spiritual level too. A reverence for nature and all living things solidifies our connection, unifying us as part of nature. If God created all things, all things are of God and part of God. There is no hierarchy, only connectedness. Once we understand this connectedness, we become more connected - and are more in line with our true nature.

This is not a religious book or a book about the existence of God. It is not meant to offend anyone or change people's religious views. If anything, this is a guidebook to strengthen your beliefs in what is really important regarding your faith. It applies to anyone who simply wants to live with greater Joy. Many people seek happiness and are looking for love. What they fail to realize is that it's an inward search. Honestly knowing yourself is the only way to truly know love and happiness. I am not here to judge. I only offer you what has strengthened me and given me direction toward living a happier, more fulfilling life. This is a book about love. Join me in my journey so you too may learn to live with greater love in your life.

Part 1

Nature's Being

Chapter 1 - God, Love & Truth

God is Love

God is the creative energy that encompasses all things. God is the source of all things. God is infinite, transcending space and time, from the most infinitely minuscule subatomic particle to the whole of the universe. God's energy knows neither yesterday nor tomorrow, only right now. Someone who does not believe in God might argue that this energy is simply the energy of all the universe, with so many atomic reactions occurring that create the stars, planets and life. You could argue that there is no reason to include God in the equation. So, why does God exist? How do you justify the existence of God?

Quite simply, God is love.

Trusting the Universe in its Unfolding Perfection

I've asked many people to name things they know to be absolutely true. Name something that is undeniably, irrefutable and cannot be open for interpretation. An absolute truth is beyond debate. Even if you don't understand it fully, you know that it simply just is. I've pondered this question for a long time and came up with two things. The first is mathematics, because numbers do not lie. You can add, subtract, multiply and divide and the answers are always absolute. The second absolute truth is love.

Nobody fully understands why, but love just *is*. Love is all things good. Love is that feeling that fills you with joy, gives you peace, and brings contentment. It is a necessity of life. It is the one thing that every person strives for. Love is a creative force that gives birth to generations and fosters community, fellowship, compassion and mutual respect. Its creative potential gives rise to amazing feats of ingenuity and imagination. It solves problems, fixes things and makes things new. If you have nothing else, love is all you need. With love, anything is possible. With love, the right decisions are instinctively made. With love, there is no conflict. No resistance.

It's interesting when I ask people to describe God and give me their perception of what God is. Their answers differ based on their faith, yet the core of what they all believe God to be is exactly how I just described love. And love is an absolute truth.

There are so many ways we feel love. Whether it's love of family, a friend, a lover, a pet, it's all the same. Poets, authors, songwriters and friends on Facebook all either sing its praises or lament its passing. There is no stronger feeling or greater attraction. No drug in the world can replace the euphoria you feel when you experience love. It is the single unifying thing in all creation that binds us to all things good. So, why does love elude us? Why is it fleeting or seem cruel at times? Does love last forever, or does it seem just out of reach? Imagine if you could always feel love. Would you if you could? The reality is, when you are living as God intends, love is the norm.

Human perception of love typically fixates on the pursuit and the search for love. We grow up believing our soulmate is out there. We often judge people we meet and qualify them as a potential Mister or Miss Right. We create degrees of love and categorize people as friends, acquaintances, and lovers. This is an outward journey, a constant search. Some of us find this love and others search their entire lives without finding it. The lucky ones turn their search inward and discover the source of Universal Love. Only then is the true meaning of love revealed.

Universal Love is love as God intends it. It is love for all things, including yourself. There are no degrees of love. There are no judgments. This love is from the source. It guides you in your thoughts and actions, removing ego's judgments and freeing you from any doubt or fear.

Your Connection

The idea of God and your connectedness to God is not complicated. Most all religions believe God created all things. Having created you, you too are part of God and are connected to all things. This connection is your spirit, your soul or whatever it is that you want to call it. God creates out of love. In God, there is only goodness. Therefore, your true nature is to be as part of God and live in love and goodness. It is that simple!

However, once you are creating contrary to love and goodness, whether it's through greed, selfishness, anger or envy, you are creating outside of your true nature. Even if you don't believe there is a God, these ideals still hold true. The concept of right and wrong is universal. We act out of love because it is the right thing to do. But, imagine if we lived in a universe where everyone was selfish and cruel. Life would suck! It would also not be sustainable. Now, imagine a world where everyone lived in love and helped each other. Life would be free of cruelty and selfishness, and we would live in peace. That is how life is meant to be.

We delight in the sensation that love gives us. There are even physical and chemical reactions that occur when we love. As conscious beings, we have been given the gift to appreciate the feelings of joy contentment, security, and belonging that love gives us. These feelings are what everyone needs most. No matter what your race, creed or country, the goodness of love, the need for love and all that it represents, is the one universal idea that we all can agree on. That is why love is the one universal truth that is beyond debate.

For me, love is God in motion. God is the creative source from which love is. "We are created out of love" is a literal term, not just a feeling. It is the foundation from which we are created. It joins all things. Love is a functioning energy we are just learning to tap into. That is why it is our true nature to live our day-to-day lives interacting with other people, working in concert with the world and the universe we are part of. Unfortunately, we as humans always seem to teeter between living our true nature and existing in an ego-dominated society.

One of the most misleading aspects of our human existence is our ability to be stuck in our human experience. We are held back by our inability to see beyond what is real to us in our daily existence. Far too often we settle for "life as we know it" being as good as it gets! We forget the infinite nature that defines all of us and lose our own ability to create. We become more easily manipulated by people and things that are outside of our nature. Even when we are struggling, we find it is easier to blame others for our condition. Drugs and other harmful distractions may help to alleviate symptoms but do not address the problems. As a result, many of us stray from our true nature. We forget about love. Our thoughts become deluded as we see the world in adversarial terms, with everyone against us. We begin reacting to circumstances, instead of being the creators of our own future. Stuck in our own physical existence, we become less trusting in the unfolding perfection of the universe, and lose our connection to God and love. This denies us from our natural-self and what it truly means to be human.

Chapter 2 - Your Physical Existence

The Bigger Picture

If you ever find yourself falling into what I call the traps of being human, such as anger, depression, or addiction, consider the bigger picture. You are part of something far greater. Your human-self is a body you occupy, a temporary corporeal existence ...But your soul? That is your connection to all things, and it is infinite. Your perception of what is real is inconsequential compared to this connection. From birth to death, your physical being is only a small part of who you really are. We all spend so much time defining our individual selves in life that we tend to overshoot the basic essence of who we are - and that is a physical manifestation of love.

As humans, we create a diverse range of emotions that make us spin out of control, never knowing how we are truly meant to feel. Our core emotion is love, our natural state of being. Yet, love is never founded in anger, and anger is never found in love. When we feel negative emotions, we separate ourselves who we are meant to be. Feeling depressed is often a reaction to feelings like fear and loneliness. Thoughts and feelings of fear or loneliness being not who we really are, can be dispelled when we embrace our infinite-self.

When you find yourself caught in these traps of being human, it's essential to your wellbeing to get back to basics and give yourself a break. Doing this, you open a window and eventually the door to self-love. When you can love yourself, love in all its forms will follow. Worries in life tend to dissipate and problems seem more manageable when you see the bigger picture. It's understanding the difference between your own physical existence here on Earth and your connection to your infinite-self, that gives you peace. The challenges you face in life today are of little consequence to someone whose true essence is infinite and eternal.

Allowing love into your life begins with you. You have the ability to look in the mirror and accept yourself as God made you, so love yourself as the perfection that created you. You were born perfect. There are no accidents in life, and everything happens for a reason. There is a very specific reason you were put on this Earth at this place and time. There are cause-and-effect circumstances that put you where you are today. You started out exactly as God intended. Are you living that intention today? If not, focus more on being you, and don't allow others to tell you that you're not up to snuff or that you don't fit the mold of their perceptions. It is people who create societies and rules. And if the people who run societies or create rules do so by being judgmental, prejudicial or self-serving, they are not creating or loving according to their own true nature.

If you are act out of love and govern yourself according to your true nature, you cannot be judged. *There is no judgment for that which is right.* Wear that on your sleeve. Embrace who you are, and let love be your mantra when you meditate. You are love. Remain modest, and don't hold grudges toward those who do judge you. Remember, they are not acting from their own true nature, and the correct way to respond is with love. Always lead by example, take the high road, and lead with love.

Taking Yourself Out of Alignment

I have dealt with addiction in my life. While I never let it draw me into a life-threatening situation, I've had my moments of unhealthy decisions. I understand the allure of alcohol, tobacco and drugs, as well as their temporary benefits and long-term consequences. I've seen that allure destroy people, and their loss is tragic. Friends of mine have been to Hell and back. I have seen it restrict other's mental and physical development. What I find most common is the ability of addictive behavior to limit people's true potential. Casual use often results in lost hours, lost weekends, and lost years for some. For the casual user, addiction becomes a crutch, part of their everyday life. Without affecting them enough to completely impair their ability to function, the addictive behavior takes the sting out of life. Many of us, including me fall into this category. I'm not going to be a hypocrite. A few drinks help to forget a bad day. A cigarette calms the nerves. Many of us have been there at some point in our lives.

A problem arises when that behavior begins to define us, becoming the norm. Let's face it, most addictive behavior is unhealthy. When it becomes a part of daily life as a means of escaping from something that is causing unhappiness, addiction only addresses the symptom and not the problem. That is a sign you are not living your true nature. I may enjoy a good glass of wine, but I can no longer binge-drink the way I did in my youth. That's not who I am anymore. And that's part of recognizing myself as who I am. I am the collection of experiences that define my past and what I've learned from those experiences. The most important thing anyone can do is recognize the addiction for what it is, be grateful you're still alive, let the past go, and move forward to find the root of what's really ailing you. That's why an inward journey to discover your natural self is so important. In doing so, you're finding out what makes you tick.

Bringing Out What's Within

Only you know exactly who your true-self is, because that person is with you every day. Your inner voice is always telling you what you need to know. Access that part of you. Sit in quiet meditation. Be with your thoughts. Think about where you are at this moment. Make a conscious decision to be honest with yourself and your feelings - but don't be part of those thoughts and feelings. See yourself through a different set of eyes. That is the meaning of detachment. Understand what your feelings are and where they come from. See everything for what it is, but tell yourself you are no longer part of it. You will begin to see your troubles from an outside perspective. This outside perspective allows you to see things the way they are, without you getting in your own way. If what you have been doing is wrong, you will see it. You'll see what causes you pain. You'll see that your fear has kept you frozen and not allowed you to take charge of your life. You'll see how what you've been doing to yourself is not healthy, and you will know what needs to be done.

Looking inward also allows you to connect with your subconscious and helps identify behaviors you may not even be aware of that stand in contrast to your true-self. Through the use of affirmations and positive recasting, you can recondition these behaviors. When I'm confronted with a bad situation and know I need to make a change, I often say, *"What's the worst that could happen? At least I have my health."* or *"I am a being of perfect health, and I choose to change for my own good."* Sometimes that is all I need to send my thoughts into a new direction, because I believe that if you have your health, you've got everything you need to be happy! When used consistently, affirmations also work to reprogram the subconscious, bringing your subconscious thoughts and beliefs in alignment with your conscious thoughts and beliefs, thus allowing you to reset the behavioral blueprint you had originally created for yourself, with new ideas and information that will better serve you today.

So, when you see your reflection in the mirror, smile at that "human being" looking back at you. See yourself only as God intended you to be, and be that person. You are a being of love, who knows only love. No judgment. No fear. Only love. This feeling will liberate you from the hardships you struggle with. Then, you can lift yourself up from your troubles and move forward toward a solution.

The Road of Life

I like to think of my life's journey as a road, a path I was intended to travel. That path is my true nature. When I am on it, I love the life I live because it's filled with love, and I am as God intended me to be. When I deviate from my path, I'm living outside of my true nature and begin to struggle. If I stray far enough from my path, my struggles turn to genuine suffering. It's often a delayed response. Some call it karma. And in the midst of my struggles, when I realize the mistake and return to my path, the suffering ends. The struggles slowly become manageable and eventually subside, because I have returned to my path. When I am on my path and acting within my true nature, a universe of opportunities begins to open to me. That's when everything starts clicking. It is an amazing feeling that must be embraced with gratitude and humility however. Otherwise, it is not sustainable.

Have you ever had this happen? Just when you think everything is going great, unforeseen problems arise suddenly, putting an end to your joyous ride. Once, I found myself riding high and everything seemed to be perfect. Someone asked me if I went to church regularly and I replied, "I don't need God, I make my own reality happen." I did indeed! Not long after that, the bottom fell out from under me. It took a long time to realize what had really happened. As they say, "Karma's a Bitch!" And, boy was it ever! My business failed, my marriage failed and I needed to navigate some deep, dark water before I could find my path again.

During that time just before the fall, I had stepped outside of my true self and allowed my ego to take control. My ego had all the answers. Even when trouble was staring me in the face, my ego said, "I got this" - and sealed my fate. I didn't understand what I know now. In retrospect, the good times I was experiencing were a direct result of the previous years when I was living my true nature. I had graduated with an Environmental Science degree in college and was trying to save the planet. I was riding the wave of good karma I had created, but my ego wanted more. I did not understand what true success really was, and I began making bad decisions. Like Icarus, I flew too close to the sun, singeing my wings when my head got too big, and I began to feel the sting of my hubris.

As the saying goes, *"When you hit rock bottom, the only way is up."* And when the dust settled after my fall, I was looking up from the bottom of a deep dark hole. What kept me going were my children. They were the light from above that gave me purpose to climb up from where I was and begin putting my life back in order by taking on the necessary work to get me back on my intended path.

The good news is you can always return to the path you are intended to be on. I know my path (my dharma) is to help people and be a steward of the Earth. I know this as plain as day, because when I am doing it, life is effortless and prosperity follows.

As you can see, my life has been a road full of ups and downs, a meandering path filled with learning lessons that have brought me to the place I am today. There is no other path I could have taken if I am intended to teach people about life. This book wouldn't exist otherwise. I needed to experience it. It's funny, because I look back on all the distractions and deviations my journey took, all the lessons learned, all the skills I have mastered, and I understand now that it all is exactly how it was intended to be.

Could I have done things differently? Absolutely, but that would have required me to wake up sooner and realize what God intended for me. It would have been a different life for sure. It's fun to speculate how things might have been, but I cannot dwell in that place or lament lost opportunities. We make decisions based on the best information we have at that time and must embrace the consequences of those decisions. As it is, I love my life, and I would not change a thing. There is only today. I am on my path, exactly where I am meant to be at this exact moment, because I am living my true nature.

When I was in college, I declared that I was going to be a teacher. I was in my early twenties, and I remember exactly where I was and who I was talking to when I said it. However, I never completed my teaching degree. Life happened. I made other decisions. I got married. I became a father, a video producer, environmental educator, a salesman and consultant. I did not take the traditional route I may have been meant to take, but I am still a teacher in the broadest and truest sense of the word. Every experience offered me an opportunity to hone my skills and prepare me to be better at what I am ultimately intended to do.

Today, I add writer and public speaker to my list. All these experiences combined to form the person I am meant to become. I visualize myself talking to large audiences, helping and inspiring people to discover their inner-selves the way I have been inspired. The universe works through me as I become an instrument of peace and love. That is the life I envision for myself. For me, there can be no other way. That is how singularly focused I am on my path.

This sense of clarity and purpose is what I want you to find for yourself. Step into your journey with your eyes, ears and heart wide open. Look deep inside yourself to find that passion that burns within you. Ask yourself if that passion is founded in love for all things, including yourself. If it is not, then that is not your true calling. If it is, then embrace it. Own it. Run with it and make it your life. You will be better for it, and the world will be a better place because you are following your calling - your true nature.

Your Infinite-Self

Perhaps the most important thing to take away from this is that your physical existence is a series of life experiences defined by the thoughts you keep and decisions you make. On the surface, it is a focused point in time. Without looking deep inside yourself, life follows a linear progression, limited to your past, present and future experiences. When you discover your true nature, you discover the infinite side of your being. With it, time is irrelevant. There is only here and now. This is your direct connection to God. This is your creative source. This is the timeless, formless self that is your soul. The energy of the universe. Heaven. The after-life. It's all the same! You are connected to all things. This is the place where all things happen at once. There is no time. No chronology of events. Endless, infinite possibilities unfold in an instant, with enough energy to create universes. With God, anything is possible.

Infinite possibilities. That's a strong statement. But the potential for creation is only limited by the imagination. That's how the unthinkable becomes possible. The moment someone thinks of it, the energy is already being created. Ideas do manifest into reality. Evidence is everywhere. We once believed the world was flat. Now astronauts can live in space, safely return home and very few people are even impressed anymore. We take for granted all the great feats of building and technology, yet someone had to conceive of them before they could be built. In nature, there are amazing designs of ingenuity as well. Spotted Jewelweed (*Impatiens capensis*), is a little spotted orange flower that grows often near water. When the flower turns to seed, the plant creates a seed pod. The plant has adapted to disperse its seeds further by using a spring mechanism in the seed pod that launches the seeds into the air when an animal walks by and makes contact. The seed pod literally explodes. Seeds hurdle two to three feet in every direction, and what you're left with is a piece of spring-shaped plant material. It's really quite fascinating and fun to play with. I love to show kids Spotted Jewelweed, because it opens them up to the wonder of nature's creation.

Your Apotheosis

My ego defines my persona and makes me Gary Pfister. I have been given a name that characterizes me as this person who walks and breathes and writes. My infinite-self is part of the universal source of all things. I've chosen to call it God, though I know it is unnamable. There are many names for God: Jehovah, Allah, Krishna, Tao, Yahweh, Elohim...the list is endless. Historically, humans have done a great job of naming things. Everything in my world has been given a name. This makes it very convenient for me when I need to ask you to pass the sugar. But in the universe of one single source of all things, everything is nameless. Chinese philosopher Lao Tzu wrote of this 2500 years ago in his 81 verses of the Tao Te Ching. He speaks of the world of ten-thousand things. It is a metaphor for a world of lots of stuff, and everything has been given a name. Yet the Tao (God), which is all things, is nameless. *"That that can be named is not the Tao."* It is the idea that once you begin to give things names, you create separation between things. Remembering that you are one with the Tao, one with God, will keep you aligned with your true-self.

Everything is part of this loving energy that we call God. We were created to create. That is our purpose. What that is for you may be different from what it is for me. Our individual purposes may vary. The single universal mind that we call God has one purpose, and that is love. We were given minds to imagine, hypothesize, formulate and lift us into action. The common thread that links your mind to mine is love. That is the creative connection you and I have.

Tapping into your creative connection is the inward journey I am talking about. Realizing your infinite-self will transform your life, effectively exposing your physical existence, your world of ten-thousand things as Lao Tzu put it, and opening your consciousness to the one source that created all things. It's a direct connection. Everyone talks about the power of prayer, well here it is. The awareness that you are connected to God and connected to all things releases the self-imposed limitations that prevent you from becoming as God intended. These blockages created from 'being human' disappear as you are connected to God, creating as God intends you to create, and living in alignment with your true-self. That is your apotheosis.

Chapter 3 - Mindfulness and Self-Awareness

Becoming Aware of Your Thoughts

How much attention do you give to your thoughts? What is your day-to-day attitude towards life? Are you happy most of the time? Is your future bright, or do the problems of the world drag you down?

You are the thoughts you keep. The things you focus on the most dictate your mood, your outlook on life, the types of relationships you have, and your acceptance of happiness. These thoughts invariably affect your cumulative life experience and your overall state of wellbeing. Your conscious mind is your awake mind. These are the thoughts that allow you to perceive, analyze and ponder what's in front of you and formulate ideas about your world. For example, I think chocolate tastes good. I like chocolate. Chocolate makes me happy. Except for a very small minority, most of you right now are in agreement with me and likely feeling a sense of pleasure at just the thought of chocolate.

Mindfulness - and being mindful - is the ability to use your conscious mind to become aware of your thoughts on a moment-by-moment basis. When you are aware of your thoughts, you can choose the thoughts to keep and the ones to let go of. Over time, the thoughts you decide to keep develop into your dominant ideas and perceptions about life, people and things. These ideas also affect your mood, your emotions, and your general outlook on life. When you think about your life, is the glass half-full or half-empty? Are you looking forward to your day? Do you like the people around you? Are you happy? All of these perceptions and decisions begin with the basic thoughts you keep.

Once an idea in your conscious mind becomes dominant, it moves and becomes locked away in your subconscious mind. It becomes a thought that you no longer need to consciously debate or think about. "Hot water will burn you. It hurts." You don't need to think about it. You just know it's true. Many of these thoughts embed themselves in your subconscious mind through experiences. As a child, I knocked a steaming hot cup of tea on myself and it burned. I don't even remember doing it because I was so young. Yet, every time I see steam, or I'm about to put my hands under a hot water faucet, I know it could burn me.

Whether absorbed quickly or slowly, these are thoughts that your subconscious mind considers to be absolutely true. So, when you're in fear or in pain and someone says to you, "Come on, it's all in your head," they are telling you to defy what your subconscious mind knows to be true. Our subconscious thoughts protect us from things that can hurt us. They can also tell us what makes us happy. When I see that chocolate in front of me, I don't need to think about it. I know it tastes good. My mouth is even salivating right now as I'm writing these lines. It's an instant reaction of my subconscious mind.

However, just because an idea is part of your subconscious does not always make it true. When I was in my youth, racism abounded in my all-white community. It was considered acceptable to make jokes about people from other ethnic backgrounds. It was socially acceptable to hate someone with a different skin color than my own. There were even books published that were filled with racial jokes, and I laughed at the humor. That learned behavior became ingrained into my subconscious mind - until one day my conscious mind woke up and I changed my thought processes. Today, that behavior is not acceptable. The idea of hatred in general is no longer part of my psyche. When I began interacting more with people of other ethnicities, I realized we were more alike than we were different. I retrained my subconscious mind to focus on respect, compassion, and love, removing notions of hate and prejudice. The subconscious mind can be retrained, and that begins with mindfulness.

Exercises in Mindfulness

Zen Master Thich Nat Hahn teaches an important lesson in his book "Miracles of Mindfulness": encouraging you to pay attention to the thoughts you keep, and always be present in the moment. He offers exercises, such as the *Mindfulness of Doing Dishes*, where I've learned to find pleasure in even the most mundane tasks. Have you ever been washing dishes, rushing to get done so that you can move onto something you'd rather be doing? You might even create anger or anxiety in your mind, because this task is getting in the way of having fun. Instead of getting upset, he suggests you try being in the moment and fully experience the process of doing the dishes. You are in the process of creation after all - creating clean dishes. Slow down your thoughts and allow yourself to get drawn into the process. Allow your motions to be done with grace rather than speed and pay attention to every movement. This exercise can be carried out with other everyday tasks as well. Exercise mindfulness when you brush your teeth, vacuum the rug, or fold laundry. All these tasks need to be done anyway, so why not do so with grace and peace of mind? Not only will you become more relaxed in your day-to-day efforts, when you are living in the moment, you begin to achieve greater communion with your thoughts. That is the benefit of this exercise.

Once I began to practice mindfulness, I created a game for myself. Every morning I'd wake up and see how long I could go thinking only loving thoughts. At first, it was not easy. I learned how quickly and how often I would get upset by something on the news, or when someone cut me off in traffic, or said something to me that was unkind. Every time I caught myself reacting out of anything but loving thoughts, I would be mindful of it, check myself, and then return to my loving thoughts. Now, I don't even think of this as a game. It's become part of my everyday life. I still get upset at times when someone cuts me off in traffic, but now I don't react the way I might have in the past. I let the feelings flow and then let them go, sending a blessing to the person who cut me off, because for all I know, they may be rushing to get to the hospital emergency room. What I have done is train my subconscious mind to exist in a place of constant love. It is a conscious effort to change misaligned behaviors I had learned in the past.

I've always been impressed by my father-in-law's ability to be cool under pressure. It's as if nothing ever bothers him. One day, he explained to me that a doctor had told him that if he didn't change his ways and not be so hot-headed, he wouldn't be around to see his children grow up. This reality check motivated him enough to change the way he perceived things in his life. He became mindful of his thoughts, mindful of the things that were causing him harm, and he changed the way he lived his life. He effectively managed to minimize problems and reduce the stress on his body.

It's amazing to consider what the mind is capable of doing when it is motivated to do so. So many of the issues and ailments that adversely affect our lives can be curtailed and even cured through mindfulness. Do you feel like your life is out of control? Slow it down. Become aware of where your thoughts originate. Take that journey inward by becoming cognizant of the thoughts that help you or hurt you. You will find that the answers to all your problems are already within you. You have the answers you need because nobody knows *you* like you do. Discover that person. Get to know your inner-self and make an honest effort get to know what makes you tick.

Mindfulness and Meditation

When making the effort to be more mindful, I cannot stress enough how important meditation is. And you don't need to take a class to learn how to do it right. Just do it! Take time out of your day, get comfortable, and quite your mind. Clear out the noise. Simply sitting in quiet contemplation will allow you to see things more clearly. It's a process of slowing down and being in the moment. Once you silence the mental noise and move beyond your conscious thoughts, past your subconscious mind, you can begin to open the connection to your higher-self, your God-consciousness. This is the part of your mind that connects to all things. Some consider this the highest state of being. The truly enlightened people in human history are said to have achieved this state.

The fact is, this higher state of being is not out of reach for you and me. On a couple occasions during my meditative practice, I have reached a place of supreme bliss. It was a feeling of absolute peace. Once I got there however, I had this "ah-ha!!" moment of realizing where I was. And sadly, in an instant, that realization bounced me right back where

I started. That's why it's call the *practice* of meditation. Until we reach that ultimate state of enlightenment, we must continually work at it. So, it's like the lottery. You can't win unless you play, and the sooner you start, the better off you will be.

The path to enlightenment begins with mindfulness and meditation. Take control of your thoughts. Center your practice in a foundation of love. Begin to remove any thoughts that do not benefit you and the world you live in, and concentrate only on ones that do. Lastly, remember that you can only control your actions alone and nobody else's, so focus on yourself. Focus on love. As you expand your meditative practice into your day-to-day routine, stay within the confines of your own thoughts and actions. Don't worry too much about what others think, say, or do. This will help keep you more centered and self-aware. Through mindfulness, you become self-aware. Only through self-awareness do you establish and maintain your connection with God.

Awareness of Your Connection to All Things

Knowing you are part of something far greater than yourself is a humbling experience. Your ego tells you that you are the center of the universe. It tells you that *you* are the most important thing in *your* life. The ego tells you, "It's all about me." If you ever find yourself thinking this way, just go outside on a clear, starry night. Look up at the stars. If you're lucky enough to be in a place where you can see the clusters of stars that form the Milky Way Galaxy, you will gain an even greater perspective. These clusters of stars form a milky haze, stretching like a glowing band across the heavens, giving the galaxy its name. In reality, this haze is the culmination of billions of stars lighting the night sky.

The Milky Way is a disk-shaped, spiral galaxy spinning through the universe. At its center are the densest clusters of stars. Along the outer perimeter of the spiral, the star clusters begin to thin out, wrapping around the center of the galaxy like the spinning blades of a fan and giving the galaxy its spiral shape. Our sun and solar system are located within one of these outer clusters, far from the center of the galaxy. From our standpoint on Earth, as we look into the center of the Milky Way, let's consider for a moment that your perspective is from the outer reaches of the galaxy looking inward. If you look in the opposite direction, you are looking out towards the far reaches of our galaxy, out beyond the Milky Way, deep into the universe. The closest star within the Milky Way is about

4.24 light years or 24.93 trillion (24,930,000,000,000) miles away from Earth. And there are countless stars and galaxies located further beyond this distant star neighbor. All of these stars combine to form the known universe that we are part of. What's beyond our universe? One can only guess. So, let me ask you, do you really believe what your ego tells you – that it's all about you?

My ego once told me I was the center of the universe. In reality, I may never actually see the center of the universe in my lifetime, but it's comforting to know it's there - and that I am part of it. It's comforting to know that I am part of something far greater than I could ever imagine. That takes the pressure off me knowing that the future of the universe doesn't hinge on what I eat for breakfast today. God created all things, and all things are part of God, so I too am part of God. We all are! And, God's creations are perfect in every way. I am different from you, yet we were both created exactly as God intended. In spite of our differences, we are both perfect in every way. There are no accidents. Every plant, animal, fungus, single-celled organism, and virus is a living reflection of God's creation, perfect in every way.

Think about this too: If we are all part of God, and all things are part of God, and you do harm to one of God's creations, you are doing harm to all things. Stepping on a bug may not bring about global collapse, but if you step on enough bugs, it certainly will. All of God's creations depend on one another for survival. Being mindful of your connection to all living things is the first step to having reverence for life. This comes in the form of respect and love. Once you have established this reverence for God's creations as part of your being, you begin making decisions that derive from your true nature.

Awareness of Your Creative Potential

Connecting with your true nature and not your ego unlocks a wide array of creative possibilities. Knowing the thoughts you keep affects the decisions you make, and focusing only on thoughts originating from a loving source, forms your connection with the loving source that creates all things. Be mindful of this connection. Contemplate this connection. Meditate on it, and adopt a mantra that says you are part of the loving creation of God and it is your intention to create as God creates.

Avoid being someone who says, "Oh, I'm not good at anything" or "I'm not creative." Creativity is one of the preordained gifts that every human being is blessed with.

The only limitation to a person's creative ability is the limitation they put on their own capacity to love.

Love is an overwhelming force that breaks through all limitations, making all things possible. When you focus your desires, set goals and act with intention that is fostered in love, you are tapping into the divine energy of that which created you. Latent forces are awakened because your loving intention is in alignment with a loving universe. It is the awareness of that loving intention that inspires your creative potential.

Once you become aware of your creative abilities, you will most certainly want to use them. Fueled by compassion and kindness, inspired by feelings of gratitude, you live your life in a constant state of giving. Intention now turns to action, and your life's purpose is realized.

"He who has a why to live for can bear almost any how."

- Friedrich Nietzsche

Awareness of Your Infinite-Self

Knowing you are part of God is to know you are not only part of something far greater than yourself. It is knowing that you transcend time itself. This brief moment you spend on Earth is but a blink of an eye to your infinite-self. We put so much emphasis on time, don't we? Time tells us when to wake up, brush our teeth, go to work, eat our meals, and go to sleep. We count the days until vacation. We hope to live a long life. When we are young, we can't wait to grow up. When we grow up, we try to hang onto our youth. Then, we begin to count the days we have left before we die.

What if I told you none of this really matters? Your infinite-self, your true-self, is timeless. Remember, we are all part of God. God is infinite, always present, always creating in a world without end, and you are part of that world too! The First Law of Thermodynamics in physics states that energy can be transferred from one form to another, but it cannot be created or destroyed. We are energy. Our soul, the essence of what we are and our connection to God is all energy. That indestructible energy is your infinite-self.

Embrace this truth in your day-to-day life by putting less emphasis on the rigors of time. Sure, if you have a dentist appointment, it's still a good idea to show up on time. But, you can stop being married to the schedule you've created for your life. I always chuckle when someone tells me about their 5-year plan. Yes, it's good to set goals and have direction, but unless your plans are in alignment with

God's creative intentions, I wish you luck. One thing I've learned in life is that nothing ever goes according to plan. The more you try to force things, the more things go wrong. Patience is the order of things. It is the pace of nature. Create within that flow, and let nature take its course.

For example, we always try to slow down when we go on vacations. Some people take up pottery or painting, because it slows them down and brings them back to their natural pace. That is the essence of mindfulness. That's the pace to use when washing the dishes or cleaning the floor. It's the little things that count, and I'm suggesting you adopt this practice in your daily life. Don't let go of the moments in between all those things you think you need to do. Do the things you need to do, and do them with as much ease as possible. You will encounter much less resistance and stress if you do. Take time to enjoy the process, and see if this doesn't take you to a happier place in your life.

Remembering my infinite-self comes in handy most often when I'm feeling my greatest stress. I've experienced some incredibly stressful events. I still find myself in situations where my former self might have folded under the pressure or acted out in a way that is not conducive to finding a peaceful resolution. Yet today, I manage to find myself more often in a place of ease. I often surprise myself with my abilities to minimize negative effects. It's a very simple process: I simply surrender to the situation. That doesn't mean giving up. I do everything I can to find a resolution, positioning myself to minimize the effects. When I've done all I can do and assessed all possible outcomes, I simply tell myself that I am not defined by the situation I am in. This is not who I am.

The truth is that I am part of something far greater that transcends all time and space. I am part of God's love, and the will of God will never take me to a place where the grace of God cannot protect me. If I am truthful and govern myself as God intends, love fills me. There may be difficult times ahead, but I've done everything I can do at this point. I am in God's hands, so let it be done and move on. In time, things get better.

The key here is how I chose to spend that time in between. If obsessive thoughts take over, I merely suffer longer. By understanding my infinite-self and existing from that timeless, loving place, I move forward with grace, focusing only on moving forward and the lesson learned. Remember, we are the thoughts we keep. By channeling thoughts away from the problem, I am once again in my creative zone. I am mindful of what is truly real. I am aware of my infinite nature. This allows me to find happiness even while I'm going through troubling times. No matter what happens, my true essence cannot be destroyed. I know that I am part of something far greater than the situation I am in, and I am safe.

I find that the more I practice this affirmation, the easier my life gets. The down times have become more manageable and occur less frequently. Having the ability to go about my day without carrying the burden of my problems, allows me to focus on what is truly important, bringing me into alignment with my higher purpose.

Awareness of Your Higher Purpose

One of the greatest lessons we can learn is that there are no accidents in life. Whatever situation you find yourself in, you put yourself there. All things happen for a reason. Truthfulness is the key to understanding this. Are you being truthful with yourself? Are you living in accordance to what really feels right to you? Do you go through life with grace and ease, or do you need to manipulate your way in life in order to get what you want? Has your "house of cards" ever fallen from the weight of the BS you're dishing out? Only when you are truthful and living a love-centered life will your situation naturally improve. It is the only way to release the karma of your life.

That's not to say that there will never be accidents that you have no control over. Typically, these events are caused by someone else who is living (or not living) their own higher purpose. These are often the karmic reactions of so many people living life amid so many moving parts in our physical world. Simply put, the more people we encounter who not living their true nature, the more ripples we must navigate in our lives. But when we are on course and aware of our higher purpose, and actively working to fulfill that purpose, the waters naturally become calmer.

There is but one highest purpose, and that is to *Be Love*. That is our universal purpose, and there are no greater purposes. It's like when I was growing up and friends would ask me to rank the best rock and roll bands. In my world, there was the Beatles, and then there was everyone else. It's the same with love. Nothing tops love. It's so simple. It's staring you right in the face, and you know it. Why would anyone not want to believe it, embrace it - and live it all day, every day?

My big question to the world is this: What would happen if everyone in unison began *being love* at the same time? I believe we would be changed forever, like having a light switch turned on. How amazing that will be, and I believe it will happen. It has to happen! Once again, it is the nature of things. When we die, we return to our infinite-self. Enlightenment is achieved. We are within God's grace. The real trick is achieving it while we're still alive.

Imagine how cool it would be if we all reached that state of being, where love was all that matters. From a biblical sense, that could be the second coming of Christ. Instead of Jesus himself returning, I believe the "second coming" is when every person on Earth begins to live as Jesus lived and as God intends. That is our higher purpose. Live in love as we were intended when God manifested us into our physical human-self.

I believe each one of us has an individual higher purpose as well. Many of us spend a great deal of time trying to find out what that purpose is. We seek. We search. We explore, but what do we really find? Often it's not the answer we're meant to find. We spend much of our lives searching for the answer in an outward direction. We fill our lives with stuff. We crave status. We follow established norms of what is acceptable and expected of us. Yet, when we look for external answers, all we create is an illusion. Only if we look hard enough *inward* do we find the answers that have been there all along. It's part of our divine programming. When we took physical being, we actually did come with a set of instructions. We just never took them out of the box. These instructions may not have been spelled out literally for each of us, but there is a common foundation. And that is love.

Once you become mindful of your creative potential, your connection to all things, and your infinite loving self, you open yourself up to discovering how you fit into this menagerie of creation. This is what makes you special. It is the true purpose for the self, apart from what the ego creates. Once you do this you now have the ability to see your part in all of this for what it is. From here, your individuality kicks in as it was intended when you came into physical form. All your special skills come into play. That great wonderful mind you possess, the only real "you," is free to expand. Ideas begin to flow. There is clarity.

For me, I do what feels right. It's that simple. This has allowed me to step out of my own way and see myself for exactly who I am. I am a teacher. I am a purveyor of knowledge and ideas. When I was younger I wanted to fly jets, but that didn't feel right to me over time. When I am in front of a classroom or a group of people, or just conversing with someone with a question, it just feels right.

Each of us needs to find our true purpose, so find yours, if you haven't already. Only you can define what that means for you. What is the one thing you truly love to do? If you know what that is, you need to act on it. Some of the greatest ideas that this world has ever known can be found in a cemetery, lost because of people's own inactivity, self-doubt, or narrow-mindedness. Don't let your own greatness die with you. It needs to be shared with the world. Know that you have a higher purpose to serve humanity and contribute to the world you are intricately a part of. The world will be a better place because you did.

Mindful of Mindfulness

By now it should be clear that mindfulness is the gateway to your inner-self. Once you open that channel, the real work can begin and you are on your intended journey. But, one thing will always get in your way, and that's you. You need to get out of your own way. Your ego wants you on autopilot, reacting to everything going on in the tangible world. Sometimes, you need to remember to be mindful, like that game I play when I see how long I can go only thinking loving thoughts. That really works on days when I'm feeling all too human, or sense I'm starting to spin a little. It's the anchor needed to bring me back to where I need to be. Meditation and contemplation are now as necessary to me as breathing, as far as I'm concerned. Only in the stillness of my quiet mind do I see things as they really are. Quiet contemplation helps me understand the feelings I am experiencing, and allows me to control the feelings instead of my feelings controlling me.

I also understand all too well that life can be really hard. Life hurts at times, but it also heals. That's why it's so important to take a mindful approach. Sometimes we only learn while we are experiencing life as it unfolds. By understanding the situation I'm in, while I'm experiencing it allows me to gain the most from it. I have found that over time, I make far fewer mistakes now than I did when I was younger, and it's rarely the same mistake twice.

Someone once told me that to become a Buddhist, I had to give up all my worldly possessions. The first thing my ego did was freak out at the thought that I had to give up all my stuff. What the person meant was that I needed to give up my *attachment* to all my stuff. Without thinking, my ego had immediately taken literally what was being said. There was a strong urge to defend and hold onto what was mine.

Well, the same goes with problems. People tend to hang onto their problems, as if they enjoy the misery they cause. Instead, why not surrender your attachment to a problem, so you can go about making things better for yourself? Be mindful of your attachment or lack of attachment to a problem. Don't let a problem define you. Be mindful of your infinite-self, your potential to create and that you are connectedness to something far greater than you or your problems. Don't allow your ego to make the problem bigger than it is. This can be paralyzing and creates a debilitating effect. Remember, the problem may be part of your journey, but it's not the journey itself. Understanding this allows you to control your emotions and become mindful of the situation as it really is - not how you've perceive it to be. With a clear head, you can find a resolution, take action, and make this episode in your life a learning lesson and nothing more.

Mindfulness of my true nature is where I like to reside most of the time. This has offered me joy even in times when there's little to be happy about. It's those nagging problems

I encounter that take me out of my bliss, and it is mindfulness that allows me to return. This same mindfulness has opened up a life of greater fortune as well. Once I started experiencing the ease and effortlessness that comes with living in the gap, good things just seemed to happen. By thinking back to when things were going well and where my mind was at that time, I could see my dilemma more for what it really was. When I follow this process today, I can see the improvement in my attitude and demeanor now. I can now see where I need to go. I make the choice to realize my bliss and embrace my loving heart with gratitude, knowing I'm on the path that is intended for me.

The way you can choose to live your life is all about perception and how you perceive your life experiences. You are the thoughts you keep, and you do create your own reality. Mindfulness expands your knowing and understanding of not just the situation you are in, but also your connection to a higher source, and your ability to *prosper* when aligned with that source. So, if you are the thoughts you keep, the clarity of your thoughts allows you to make the best decisions that ultimately decide that course your life will take. The thoughts you keep have the ability to connect you to the infinite spiritual side of your being, giving you all the necessary inspiration to reach your true potential. An inspired choice made in your life, transitions the potential reality of a thought originating from the spiritual world - into the real world of doing. All of the collective choices you make, decide the course your life will take. Your life is defined by a journey of choices.

Chapter 4 - A Journey of Choices

Stasis and Motion

The choices you make set ideas into motion that forever change whatever possible future you might have planned – or otherwise not planned. The universe works in two ways. It's constantly changing, ever-evolving, and there's an infinite number of moving parts. And then there's stasis, that state of inactivity, equilibrium and balance. Homeostasis in nature is when there is balance in an ecosystem and all plants and animals are consuming and reproducing at a balanced level. In your body, your cells are in homeostasis when all of your organs and body functions are in working order.

You, yourself might feel like you've reached homeostasis when things are going really well for you. You're riding high. Your needs are met. You've got it good, right? What more do you need to do? But the feeling never lasts does it? Why is that? Everything was going so damn good and, just like that, things change and it's gone! The reality is the illusion of achieving a balanced life never existed. There is no endgame where you live happily ever after. You thought you had arrived and stopped moving. You stopped evolving. You had no answer when asked, "What more do I need to do?" You thought you had achieved all there is to achieve, and you were content. So, once inactivity became your choice, you got swallowed up, because the universe is always in motion. It kept moving without you. There is no such thing as "stasis" in life. An object cannot remain motionless or achieve balance when the rest of the universe is pushing on it. It is like riding a surfboard. To maintain balance, you constantly need to be adjusting yourself to the changing waves.

Choice precedes action. The choices you make determine outcomes, but it doesn't end there. Even an outcome is a temporary state, a fixed moment in time. Once it has past, everything continues to change. Change is not always easy to see, yet change is always happening. Mountains grow and eventually erode away. We rarely see it happening, but that doesn't mean it's not so. The universe is perpetually in motion, and we are part of it. We exist within the ebb and flow of creation, the synergistic effect of all things happening at once. On Earth, ecosystems evolve through the interaction of species and an ever-changing environment. Geography changes and climates change. The universe keeps expanding. Our world corkscrews through the heavens, never passing through the same coordinates of space or time twice. Once we understand this, and pay attention to the cycles of change and the intricate timing of the changes that are occurring, we can better navigate our way through life and make better choices.

Allow your imagination to create your future, and never stop evolving. That's progress in a nutshell. The past is for understanding where you came from and what worked and didn't work at that time. Apart from that, it has no bearing on the present. The future is only ideas and potential. There are limitless possibilities for the future you create. Once a choice is made, your life is instantly redirected toward the possibilities that choice created. The future you are about to create is inspired by the choices you are making now.

The Life You Choose

In 1989, I was one of the youngest video editors in the city of Chicago. After graduating high school, I figured there were two paths my life could take - music or film production. I chose film production because it seemed the more likely of the two professions to find work in. So I went to film school. I remember the encouragement I received from family and loved ones after I made that decision. My father was the most supportive. He would do whatever it took to get me to the train station so I could get to school on time. I learned a lot but was a distracted student. With so many things going on outside of class, I became anxious.

I stayed in college just long enough to get the video experience needed to find work. Then, I started my own company. In the mid-1980's, VHS camcorders were becoming commonplace, so I purchased a camera and a couple video recorders and began to videotape and edit weddings. That got me a job at one of Chicago's premier video production and event staging companies. Starting at the ground floor, I quickly worked my way up to the assistant editor position and was being groomed for the editor's chair. Having just turned 23, I had a promising future ahead of me.

Then something happened that changed my life forever. One day while taking a coffee break with a client, I began to pour coffee into Styrofoam cups. The client quickly stopped me and said she didn't want to use Styrofoam. So, I poured her coffee into a mug and asked her why. That question changed my life. She explained how the production of Styrofoam released CFCs (chlorofluorocarbons) into the atmosphere, with holes in our planet's ozone layer expanding as a result. I was fascinated. Something inside me awakened and I had to learn everything there was to know about our planet and the environment.

I eventually left my position as video editor to complete my bachelor's degree in Environmental Studies, with a concentration in Ecosystem Biology and Environmental Education. I never felt more in sync with my nature of being than I did when I was doing my studies and working in that field. That life-changing event in the company break room presented me a new choice that altered the course my life would take.

For better or for worse, I was set on a path I needed to be on, flying by the seat of my pants. People thought I was crazy for leaving such a promising video editing career. Yet, quintessentially divine influence was at work here. I have no doubt about that. I had mastered my skills in video production, giving me a vehicle to communicate. And now I was being given the information and the voice to communicate a story I am meant to tell.

Looking back to the time before I even had a clear vision of what I wanted to do, I was taking classes in public speaking, oral interpretation, and acting that have prepared me to speak in front of crowds of people. I don't know what compelled me to take those classes. At the time I guess I did it for fun. Yet the choices I was making were subconsciously preparing me for what God intended for me since before I was ever born.

What Compels You

Even as I write this book, I don't even know if it will be a success or if anyone will even read it. I only know that it is something I must do. The compulsion is so strong, the vision so focused, that I know there is purpose in my choice to write it. But wait! Who am I to write this book? I've never written a book before! I have no credentials or letters after my name to make me important. I have no celebrity status. Yet, here I am. I have managed to break all the bonds my ego has created that tell me I can't or shouldn't write this book, and continue to write as if my life depends on it. That's how strong this compulsion is.

Find what compels you the same way. What have you known about yourself your entire life that you've not acted on? What drives you to the most joy? Don't say money, because money is only a means to get there. Instead, ask yourself, "Where is there?" What do you see yourself doing? Does it feel natural to you when you're doing it? Is it originating from your loving-self? This last question is an important one. If what you envision is not originating from a place of love, it's not going to feel natural, especially once you strip away your ego's desires from your list of options. Once you know what it is that you need to do, choose to take action.

I remember my mama saying to me when I was growing up, "Be bold and mighty power will come to your aid." My mom was my "motivational speaker" at the time, and she was so right. When you choose to be in alignment with your true purpose, mighty power *will* come to your aid. That power is divine. It is the fuel you need to achieve your purpose. Since I've started writing this book, things have become easier for me. More income has come to me from unlikely sources. Life is more manageable than it ever was prior to knowing and living my dharma, my chosen purpose. Some call it the law of attraction. The greatest benefit for me is the peace of mind I receive walking this path and living this life. Some call that faith. I call it your Nature of Being.

Faith in Action

The Nature of Being is a verb. It is an action. Where faith is a thought, a belief, a mental construct, the Nature of Being is the follow-through required to strengthen and fortify that faith. Faith alone may falter. Unless you put that faith in motion and live by what you know to be true, you leave yourself open to doubt, apathy, and the consequences of inactivity. Like I said, the universe is always in motion. Always creating. When faith is in alignment with God's creation and you take action, you too will create.

With God, all things are possible, so your Nature of Being allows you to release your latent creative potential, realize your true purpose, and become aligned with the vibrational source of all creation. This is the pathway to your higher self, the part of you that is connected to God. In your day-to-day human existence, you make choices that are typically reactions to stimuli in the world around you. When you are living your Nature of Being, you are dictating your own life. Action replaces reaction. That is the difference between saying you have faith and living your faith in accordance to your Nature of Being.

My Own Heaven

I was raised in a Catholic household and spent most of my early years in turmoil and fear. I was afraid that my actions and deepest, darkest thoughts would condemn me to an afterlife of fire and brimstone. Lying in bed and praying for

God to forgive me for my slightest indiscretion, I envisioned demons rising from under my bed, wrapping their arms around me, and pulling me down into the fiery abyss. I was scared of my own shadow and spent many sleepless nights hiding under my covers.

Then one day, I came to the conclusion that I was not such a bad person. I decided I wasn't going to walk on eggshells my whole life, hoping and praying that, when I died, I would be welcomed through the pearly gates. Instead, I adopted the notion that Heaven is right here on Earth and is realized in the life I would choose to live. I would simply live my life with love, focusing all of my energy on doing good in the world. In contrast, people who are criminals and bring harm to others, well, they are living their own personal Hell.

When you consider that we are all created out of goodness and love by God, what we really are is just a physical manifestation of the infinite loving energy of that intention. Therefore, the concept of Heaven and Hell can only exist when we are in our physical human form. The way you choose to live your life will decide where you reside. You can choose your level of happiness, peace, and contentment the same way you choose to suffer and struggle. You can be happy with nothing or possess all the riches in the world and still not be content. In the end, we return to God. Like a raindrop falling into an ocean, our soul returns to join again with the energy of creation.

Knowing joy is one side effect of love. Expressing and giving love to others automatically triggers joy in both the recipient and the giver. A chemical reaction actually takes place in our bodies when this occurs. Our attitude changes. We function on a higher plane of existence than we would if we were argumentative or hateful. Consequently, love is how we are meant to function. The motion of the universe is partly that exchange of love between beings.

You can always choose to be part of that loving energy, regardless of your situation or disposition. Always move to the light. Choose the light. Far too often, people allow their situation to dictate their mood, their wellbeing, and the choices they make. Learn to let your problems go and do not let them define you. Do what's best to make things better, then put your trust in God and move into a more loving state of mind. When you do this, you clear your path for joy and happiness. And with an open mind and an open heart, you attract the creative energy to create your own Heaven.

We all have a path we are intended to follow. Based on my own experience, I know this to be so. I've only struggled in life when I've moved off my intended path. The further I moved away, the more I struggled. When I went completely off-course, I've suffered, feeling the pain of my own living Hell. It's as if my struggles were God trying to nudge me back on my path. When I strayed further, God gave me a loving shove. The further I got off-course, the harder the shove - and sometimes it hurt. Each time I returned to my path, the suffering and struggling went away, and another lesson was learned.

Lessons Learned

I can't even attempt to count the mistakes I've made in my life, big and small. It would be easier to count the lessons I learned as a result. When I was younger, I used to cut my finger all the time in the kitchen. Whether I was peeling potatoes, cutting apples, or slicing carrots, I always managed to draw blood. When I got older, I finally realized that if I moved my finger out of the path of the blade, I minimized the chance of cutting myself. It was a simple lesson, maybe even obvious to you, but a lesson learned all the same. Luckily I never cut myself too badly or lost a finger, but it did take quite a few accidents to finally become conscious of the solution.

Accidents happen and mistakes are made, and bad choices are typically the reason for them. Part of being human is making mistakes and learning from them. Truly, nobody is perfect when it comes to choices. It's a part of life and growing up. The choices you make after you make a mistake are what define your maturity, wisdom, and character. When you learn from your mistakes and take action to rectify them, and do your best to make sure they never happen again, you grow in maturity and wisdom. When you take ownership of a mistake and clean up your mess, the honesty you express shows the world what type of person you are.

Thinking with Your Heart

Do you ever wish that you could go back in time, knowing what you know now? When I think about it, I imagine all the things I could change and do differently. That however, is both impossible and an unhealthy exercise of living in the past. In reality, I only have right now, so I choose to reflect back on my mistakes and own them. I give them love, because they are part of my life experience. I am the person

I am today in part because of them. I keep the lesson and release the pain. I am content with the wisdom of my life.

One of the greatest lessons I've learned is that I can avoid making bad choices by thinking with my heart. Your mind can get you out of all sorts of trouble! You can scheme up ways of manipulating a situation, deny your accountability, or hide the truth. But where does that get you? Typically it gets you into more trouble. You're just prolonging the inevitable karma that's to come.

When you think with your heart, your choices tend to be in greater alignment with the truth. You're drawing from your true nature, and being honest with yourself and other people is a natural byproduct. The result is a release from your karma. You begin to remove the resistance that is blocking your path. You gain peace of mind. There is no peace in deception and dishonesty. Once you tell a lie, you must constantly live that lie. This takes you away from your true nature. Unless you own up to the truth, you will always carry that karma with you.

Thinking with your heart allows you to make choices that originate from your honest loving-self. When you take action based on these choices, it's called taking the high road. It's not always a popular choice. Your ego wants you to avoid the pain and discomfort that is sometimes associated with it. However, the high road will always lead to greater peace, clearer vision, and less resistance in your life.

Chapter 5 - Taking the High Road

You Can't Beat the View

What does it mean to take the high road? From a literal perspective it means to take a path that first climbs upward. In the beginning, the going gets difficult. The longer the road winds upward, the greater the strain. This road will test you, and you will find out what you're made of. But as you rise higher, the high road offers a far better view of where you once came from. In figurative terms, when you take the high road, you are able to see any situation for what it is, allowing you to make better decisions. You're not being better than anyone else. You simply have a clearer perspective, and can make better choices based on facts and not only feelings or reactions. The high road offers you the ability to see what is right and really needs to be done.

For me, taking the high road is doing the right thing. A fully enlightened person would do the right thing all the time. It would be part of their day-to-day belief system, driving and defining their actions. This person would never be swayed by their ego, get offended by an insult, or make a decision based on anything other than what's morally right and for the best of all those involved. He or she would find it more productive to work toward a solution than to exacerbate a problem. Trusted to always do the right thing, the enlightened person is the ultimate diplomat and teacher.

How many people can say they do the right thing 100% of the time? Haven't we all done something in our lives that was in some way selfish? Little children mostly act according to what's best for them and don't mind making other children cry to get their way. It's not until we get older that we realize the value of diplomacy. We realize that getting along and cooperating is far more beneficial than being confrontational. Anyone who has a successful marriage can attest to that. But it's more than just give and take and having good negotiating skills. When you take the high road, you are making the right decision *naturally*. You are always right, because you don't mind being wrong. I know that sounds crazy. But when you know you are wrong and choose not to act on your judgments, offering instead to do what's right, you let go of your ego's need to always be right and end up doing what's best for all involved. That's taking the high road.

Elevating Your Intention

When I went through my divorce, there were many ways the scenario could've gone down. All the elements for a knockdown, drag-out fight were there. Like many divorces, there was anger, animosity, and betrayal on both sides. At times, I wanted to do bad things. My ego was badly bruised, but something kept telling me that the only way I was going to be able to move forward was to take the high road. This prompted me to take a good look at myself and be accountable for my actions. I began to take note of what was really important without getting caught up in the emotions of it all. Elevating my intention, I put my children's well-being ahead of my own and work peacefully with their mother towards a more productive path for us all. Instead of engaging in an outward battle, I intensified my inward journey. I knew I had made mistakes. For the first time in my life, I faced my faults head-on, owned up to them, and understood them. That enabled me to learn how to improve the choices I make and actions I take moving forward.

I also surrendered my shame along with any need to defend myself or my actions. In the process, my old-self died. I can tell you today, that guy no longer exists. I am no longer the person I was prior to my divorce. That's what happens when you take the high road, let the past go, and exist only in the here and now. By no longer reacting with my mind, I began to think and speak from the heart, doing my best to reserve judgment. I also came to know full well that people who feel a need to judge me do not define the person that I am. And the ability to forgive others becomes a natural side effect. You don't even think about it. It just happens. Taking the high road allowed me to let the past go and move on.

> *"There is no strain in doing God's will*
> *as soon as you recognize that it is also your own."*
>
> - A Course in Miracles

It's a humbling experience. Taking the high road is to deny your ego any opportunity to be right. When you stop being offended by things people say or do, and only give your energy to the thoughts originating from your natural, loving self, you become more stable on your life's path. When you are on your path, you are less likely to be openly criticized, confronted, or attacked. If you've done nothing wrong, the truth is on your side. If you've made a mistake, you own up to it and make it right.

In time, you'll find that the only one's people who are attacking you are those who resent your peace. That attitude is often coming from the minds of people whose ego can't stand the fact that you won't engage them in their conflict. The attack on you is more of an attack on themselves, because they don't like the person they see in the mirror and need to destroy anything that threatens their ego's self-justification.

Elevating your intention naturally creates a deep-seated feeling of contentment from doing the right thing. As a result, the majority of people you meet will gravitate toward you, because they sense you can be trusted. They feel comfortable around you, because you see the best in them and do not judge their shortcomings. Your less confrontational attitude and happy outlook on life naturally brings joy to others. That's because you feel better about yourself and tend to be more compassionate and giving as a result.

Knowing Nobility

A community based on cooperation owes its success to the basic fundamental principle of taking high road. It's the honor system. It's all about doing the right thing. Many problems in today's world exist because of a breakdown of this principle. People don't feel they can trust other people. They don't trust the government or law enforcement. At the highest level, politicians lie, cheat, and create conflict right in front of us on television. And society disintegrates.

The word "nobility" often refers to kings and monarchies. The root of the word is 'noble'. Individuals who run a city, state, or country are entrusted to be noble and to do the right thing. Without nobility, government will fail from the weight of its own corruption. The masses will only tolerate hardship for so long. Sadly, the discontent of the masses breeds more corruption. The disregard for the truth at the highest level trickles down into communities, neighborhoods, and families. Criminal activity becomes more commonplace and even accepted, as organized crime takes hold of communities. The irony is that communities are now turning against the police, as law enforcement is viewed as abusive, corrupt, and untrustworthy. So, you can't trust the criminals and you can't trust the police force. Who can you trust?

The strength of a society comes when the people maintain their individual integrity, even in the face of corrupt leadership. Individuals must become their own leaders and take the high road in their own lives. This means not allowing people who demonstrate immoral behavior to be the example you follow. Instead, you are noble and trustworthy so that you set an example for others. Always take the high road, so they can see you and learn to emulate you. That is how trust and respect are earned. That is how leaders are born.

Trust can be built through individual acts of truth and honor. I'm convinced that people deep-down want to be good. We want to be trusted, and there is comfort in trusting others. Nobody wants to go through life alone. We all need someone we can lean on. We want to be able to confide in others, and we are better as a society when we work together. Each of us is better off with a society on the rise, as we lift each other up. At this pinnacle of the high road, we are all elevated to the highest levels of caring, compassion, giving, and love.

Not Being So Insulted

When I knew I wanted to be a writer, I had to consider what my platform would be. I'm very passionate about many things. Do I take the activist's role on social media and alert the world to impending problems? Do I attempt to rally the troops? Or, do I simply talk about what I know and how I live my life according to principles founded in love, and allow people to decide for themselves?

There are many passionate people using their voice on the internet. I'm shocked at how nasty they can be towards one another. It's sad to see adults abusing each other, sounding more like squabbling kids in a sandbox. I believe people need to be made aware of problems, and God gave me a very loud voice for such a task. I've gotten caught up in some debates myself, but through divine intervention, I have been shown that truth often lies somewhere in the middle and that cooler heads always prevail. I still follow social media threads to keep my finger on the pulse of conversations but rarely engage in debate anymore.

I prefer quiet wisdom. More importantly, I am centered in love. Love is not about engaging in the hateful speech or allowing myself to be insulted when someone assaults my beliefs. If I know what I believe is true and have done my research, then I am content in my knowing. I also keep an open mind by reminding myself that I don't need to be right all the time. If I see the world in a certain way, and someone opens my eyes to a better point of view, I'm willing to look at and listen to what they say. That is a sign of respect for others as well as the truth.

If you seek the high road, learn to not be offended by what others say or think of you. That is more than having thick skin. It's the ability to see things with an open mind, knowing that a quiet mind will see things as they are.

A little research and due diligence never hurts either. A mind clouded in anger and lacking genuine knowledge often makes poor decisions!

I'm concerned about our world, its people, and our environment, but I also have to believe that the sun will rise again tomorrow in spite of us and our problems. I have faith in people to eventually make the right decisions. The activist in me will never die. We all must be teachers for each other. The more we work together toward peace, the more I'm convinced that it isn't necessary to thrive on the paranoia and fear that causes us to be so nasty towards one another. The first step is to look past the fear, take the high road, and begin trusting one another. Trust is earned, after all.

Choosing to Do What is Right

In my youth, I wasted a lot of energy trying to manipulate situations to get what I wanted, even when I knew my actions could be wrong. This usually resulted in short-term gains, but in the long run, my conscience was at battle with my ego and I knew what I was doing *was* wrong. My thoughts and desires were not in alignment with my true nature. Every bad decision has a cost. Every action sets in motion a dozen consequences, creating a ripple effect.

When your gains are at the expense of others, the injured party may feel forced to react. And if they act out in a similar fashion, the cycle of hurt continues. Respect and reverence for others is lost.

At some point, we all need to do what's right. The cycle of discontent needs to be broken, so our attention can be focused on greater things. All of our untapped potential is lying dormant, waiting to be released upon the world. We need to begin to expand as the universe expands. Otherwise, the pools of creativity and potential will remain stagnant.

Taking the high road is a natural progression to discovering your natural state of being. In fact, it's hard to say which comes first. The high road is part of your Nature of Being, both a place and an action toward becoming who you are meant to be. It is part of our journey in life and a choice of paths to take. For many of us, our ego has been doing the driving for most of our lives, competing with our true nature to maximize our own personal gains. That's very evident in all the discord we see around the world today. It is chronicled in our history books, and a learned behavior that has almost become instinctive. The inward journey to discover our natural-self is paramount to moving forward as we all were intended. With a mind opened to nobility, trust, and compassion, we will discover who we were truly meant to be.

Chapter 6 - Understanding Your Natural Self

Who's to Judge?

On January 7, 2015, two masked gunmen entered the office of the Charlie Hebdo Magazine in Paris and killed twelve people in retaliation for perceived insults made by cartoonists and journalists about the prophet Muhammad. In the end, a policewoman and both terrorists were also killed. The world was devastated. The outcry on social media was enormous, and I got caught up in it. In anger, I challenged the Muslim community to control their people and help put a stop to the barbarism. The responses from two of my friends really caught me by surprise. My one friend, who is Muslim, insisted that the two assailants were not real Muslims and that the Muslim community did actively denounce the attack. Another friend also called me out, telling me that I was being judgmental and not living up to my own spiritual beliefs. Coupled with the anger and sorrow, I now found myself feeling thoroughly confused. I prayed to God to show me the lesson here. What happened next changed my way of thinking for the rest of my life.

Two months before Charlie Hebdo, I had begun research on *The Nature of Being* and was reading *A Course in Miracles* when the shootings occurred. I asked God to give me wisdom and opened *A Course in Miracles* to where I had left off a few days before. These were the first words I read:

"Because I will to know myself, I see you
as God's Son and my brother."

It then went on to say:

"The alertness of the ego to the errors of other egos is not the kind
of vigilance the Holy Spirit would have you maintain."

The answer was there staring me right in the face. This wasn't the first time this had happened to me while reading *A Course in Miracles*. In fact, it still happens quite often. I will be seeking a spiritual answer, open the book, and the answer reveals itself. On this occasion however, my answer was so concise and instantaneous that I burst into tears.

What those words told me is that we are all brothers and sisters on this planet, regardless of our creed or religion. They also revealed that my judgment of the two shooters, as heinous as their actions were, made me no better than they were in terms of being my natural self.

My ego had felt like it was being attacked, and in its humanness, lured me outside of my true nature. My judgments and my actions were not founded in love. I needed to see the two men as they really were.

When they were born, the two shooters were not bad people. Jaded by hatred, they became "terrorists" when they sought to do harm to others. They were reacting to insults that their egos could not let go of. Their insult turned to hatred, and that hatred turned to murder. They abandoned their natural self, acting completely under their ego's control, and committed the ultimate sin that a person can inflict on another human being. What these men did was wrong. But while they were not living the life they were meant to live, they were still my brothers in the eyes of God. Therefore, I cannot judge. It was a tough lesson to learn, but in an instant, I no longer saw these two men as my enemy. They were just my brothers who had lost their way.

We only have control of our own thoughts and actions, and that should be our only concern as we let love (the essence of our true nature) guide us. Condemnation and judgment only fan the flames of hatred. I knew then that I had to take the high road and be a teacher, leader, and beacon of love for others to follow. That's how *The Nature of Being* became all about understanding and realizing your natural self.

We are infinite beings connected as one to the universal source that is God. We all come from the same God and yes, we all pray to the same God. A person may see them self as more special than others, but that thought comes from the ego, not their true self. The natural self has nothing to prove and never needs approval. Only kindness and love are its motivation.

Judgment occurs when your ego creates separation between you and others. It causes you to believe that you are different or better. It also makes you believe that you are constantly under attack. Things you own become *your stuff*, and everyone wants to take *your stuff* away from you. Things people say about you become insults. From these feelings of fear and separation, your hatred is aroused - and hatred only breeds more hatred. The men who shot up Charlie Hebdo acted out of hatred, and they got hatred back in kind. The fact is, any feeling you have will attract more of the same. So, whether you feel love or you feel hatred, you invite more of that feeling into your life.

When you are honest with yourself and begin to understand your ego and all its shortcomings, you can begin to tell the difference between your ego and your natural self. You can then choose which part of your consciousness gets the most attention. You can choose to focus on fear, hatred, and separation. Or you can embrace feelings of love, kindness, and compassion.

Forgiveness can be a difficult choice when someone has wronged you or hurt you badly. It's also difficult to comprehend what would compel a person to commit a heinous act. When I think of the Charlie Hebdo gunmen, I can't help to wonder what inner greatness was forever lost once they allowed hatred to control their lives. I hope they found peace in death, and with that, I give them my love. That is what it means to forgive. To forgive is to surrender all judgment. To surrender all judgment is one step towards discovering your natural self.

Hatred is Not an Option

Some people might not see the logic in what I'm saying. To forgive and to even love a murderer is preposterous, right? If it sounds crazy, it's because your perception is based on what the ego is telling you. Remember that your natural self derives from the essence of God, who knows only love. You can't have it both ways. You cannot love one person and hate another. That notion is inconceivable in Heaven. Why would it be acceptable here on Earth? Hatred exists only because we allow it to. Far too many people live under their ego's control. There are a lot of people doing bad things. This creates a cycle of cause-and-effect reactions to all the hurt being dished out. It does none of us any good if we all throw our hands up and say, "If you can't beat 'em, join 'em." Hatred is not an option. Life is not sustainable under those conditions. That is why you are called to be the change.

> *"So in everything, do unto others*
> *what you would have them do to you..."*
>
> *- Matthew 7:12*

What I am saying here isn't anything new, so why is it being disregarded by so many people? Your Nature of Being is your moral compass to "be" the person you were meant to be. When Jesus said, "I am the way and the truth and the life," he was not saying we needed to worship him. He meant for us to "be" like him! It doesn't matter which club you belong to. The Christian club doesn't believe in God any better than the Muslim club or the Jewish club. Nobody needs to join or become anything. In God, we are all one. Human beings have created these exclusive clubs and somehow feel a need to say that this club or that club is the only way to go – with non-members not welcomed in Heaven. But, that's only a great victory for the ego. However, I do not see this attitude going away anytime soon, so it's important that we all respect one another's beliefs. Do unto others with respect. If you're Christian - great! If you're Muslim - great! If you're living by the fundamental truth of your religion, and that is LOVE for all things, you are living your Nature of Being.

Does It Feel Right?

When we become honest with ourselves, we begin to think and act as our natural self. While your ego would have you make choices based on what's best for you alone, now you have a choice. One way to circumvent any debate is to honestly ask, "Does it feel right?" Forget about what you think. How does it make you feel? If you feel anything but good, it's probably not the right choice. Your natural self always wants to do what's right. It moves greed and vanity aside and downplays personal gain.

This can be uncomfortable at times. The right decision for you isn't always the popular one, because your ego will always tell you that self-preservation is more important than doing what's right. Yet, when you allow your ego to call the shots, and you choose something contrary to what is right, you set in motion a karmic series of events that typically doesn't end well. It's like the chronic liar who lied once and now must perpetuate the lie with more lies.

Once you decide to be honest with yourself, and make choices based on what's best for all, you begin to experience less resistance in your life. When you are faced with an uncomfortable situation, ask yourself what's the worst thing that could happen by being honest? If you've done something wrong and decide to cover it up, you're already dealing with the negative karma that got you to your current state. Making the decision to perpetuate that karma invites more of the same. By perpetuating the lie, you start to accumulate more and more baggage into your life. Only by being honest and doing the right thing are you able to release that bad karma and allow for good karma to enter your life. Pay now or pay later. That is the ultimate decision. You cannot have it both ways. Nobody can carry the burden of bad decisions without ultimately feeling its repercussions.

Truth is the only right answer. Without it, you need your ego to justify your actions, and this creates conflict. Where there is conflict, there is resistance. To live in peace is to live without resistance. With so many people and institutions already imposing conflict and resistance on you in life, why would you choose to bring more upon yourself? Truth relieves you of self-imposed resistance. Not only that, it shields you from the resistance created by others. The truth cannot be attacked, because there is nothing to defend! Truth is truth. There are no degrees of truth. There is nothing to justify. When you exist from a place of truth, you feel relief from all the resistance in your life.

The Heart Knows

When you make a decision based on how it makes you feel, that gut feeling you have is your natural self, who instinctively knows the right answer. This is what is meant by thinking with your heart and not just your mind. When you think with your heart, you do what feels right, without needing to justify your decision. This is so important when it comes to career decisions and marriage.

Have you ever heard someone say they took a job because it pays well, or "I married him because my dad really likes him." These are justifications. While it very well might be a great job, or he could be the right guy for you, decisions that need justification may also be absolutely wrong for you. It comes down to what your heart is telling you. There is a place for analytical thought in any decision. It's good to weigh the pros and cons, but be careful to recognize when you are misusing them to justify your actions. You must ultimately follow your heart. This is your connection with your divine source guiding you on your path. When you trust in this guidance, the right decisions come naturally.

Making decisions with your heart also reduces the amount of resistance you experience in life. You achieve greater peace, which brings greater joy. Feelings of joy, happiness, and contentment are the natural state of your being. They are byproducts of love itself. Your natural self is your loving self. Regardless of your physical condition or your surroundings, you cannot help but feel joy because you, and your choices, are one with God.

That's why the way you feel is a barometer for how closely you are aligned with your natural self. Feelings like hatred, envy, and fear are a clear indication that you've lowered yourself into your ego's false reality. You feel resistance. Anything that works to limit your joy is detrimental to your wellbeing.

When you feel love for all things and all people, you can remove those limiting feelings and your wellbeing improves. Let love dictate your thoughts before you take any action. Trust what your heart has to say. Ask yourself if it feels right. If a choice feels right, it is right, because love is truth.

Always Love

There can be only love, because in the afterlife, there is only love. When you hear stories of near-death experiences, they all have one thing in common. Every person who comes back talks about a place where there is a feeling of absolute love and nothing else. There are no choices to be made, no right or wrong, no good and evil. This makes perfect sense after all. God is the embodiment of absolute love. When we die, we return to God. We return to the perfect and pure loving energy that created us.

Here on Earth, you are that loving perfection in physical form. That is the essence of your natural self. Your potential for love is limitless, but as I mentioned before, we have been given a choice whether to use that potential or not. As human beings we have been given this choice, perhaps so that we can tell the difference and learn what love is. But in the end, there can be only one answer. If God is love and we are part of God, then we too are love and are meant to love.

When you embrace love, you embrace your loving self. When you understand this fully, knowing there are no degrees of love and love is absolute - and then follow through and be that love - you will have mastered God's lesson. You will understand your natural self by being your natural self *always*. There will be no need for judgments, no more steps to take or lessons to learn. There will be no difference between "you" and "me." There will be only "we." To exist totally in this understanding is to achieve enlightenment.

I know I'm not fully enlightened because I still hang onto who I am. After all, I like me. I'm fun to be around, but I still tend fixate on things that make us different. As much as I try, with all the work I've put in, I still catch myself making judgments of people – like with the Charlie Hebdo tragedy. And it is still engrained in our cultural psyche to see someone as attractive or not, more or less intelligent, rich or poor. In most cases, my judgments are based on whether I see someone as good or bad. Some of this is primal instinct. Some of it has cultural influence. My challenge is coping with close to 50 years of programming and reversing the beliefs that keep me from being enlightened. That is my practice. I've come a long way, but there is still work to be done.

When I find myself slipping into judgment, I tell myself is to *always love*. That simple reminder has given me the ability to tell the difference between when I'm being my natural self and when I'm not. The ability to make this distinction makes all the difference. Without it, my ego would keep me blind to the oneness of all things. When I get past all the differences, I see the perfection of God's creations. There is only love.

"Practice makes perfect" is an interesting phrase. Some say practice only makes improvement. I say we are already perfect, and practice simply allows us to realize this. That is what the term "God realization" means. Or as I like to call it, "God actualization," because we not only realize that we are as God intended us to be, but that we are actually becoming as God intends us to be.

The key is to love. Always love. Why do you think love feels so good? We always gravitate to things that make us feel good, so why would we have it any other way? Love is the greatest addiction. If your goal is to find enlightenment, or more happiness, or to better yourself in some way, start with love. Love always and completely - without measures or degrees, or conditions or consequences. Love all things and all people. In my experience of doing this, I have witnessed the negative aspects of who I am wither away as my soul awakens. This is still my practice, but I understand my perfection. Enlightenment is achieved through love. Perfection is love. Love always. Always love.

Understanding Your Infinite Being

We measure our existence here on Earth as a linear timeline from birth to death, yet our natural self is as infinite as the source energy that created us. We are manifested here into physical form for a brief moment in time to learn and to teach. We know very little about the true nature of our physical existence or the universe we are part of, so we've got our work cut out for us. There are a lot of ideas out there, but no one can be certain. What we do know is energy and matter cannot be destroyed. It can only become something else, so the universe continues to evolve infinitely. Things are born and then die, created and destroyed, but the essence of what they are continues to be recycled over and over through time.

We too continue to evolve, both physically and spiritually. The process is constant and seems never ending. Our bodies will die and return to the elemental mix of reality and our spiritual selves move onto the next phase of our infinite existence. Throughout our lives, we evolve mentally as well. We are born with inherent knowledge, instinctively knowing things about our natural self, yet we become socialized by people and our surroundings and some of this knowledge gets lost. We move through the morning, afternoon, and evening of our lives, and all the while our thoughts and perceptions change. What we valued as truth yesterday is valued less today, and by tomorrow we will have evolved into even newer ways of thinking.

When I was young, I never considered life beyond age 40. As I got closer to that age, I was even a little surprised that I had made it that far. Since then, as I'm heading into middle age, my spiritual awareness increases more and more every day. Interestingly, as this awareness grows, I think less and less about my own mortality, contrary to what you might expect. The old paradigm of the elderly person reflecting back on his life and counting the days till he meets his maker seems distant now, not just from a time standpoint, but also with regard to the value of my legacy as well. I realize that this life is not the end-all-be-all life for me.

From what I can tell, when we die we continue being who we are. Yet we all derive from the infinite spirit of God's creation. When we die, God's creation returns to its creator. I'm not going to add the "to stand in judgment" part, because God is not a man and there's nobody guarding the gate with a long list of all the bad things I've done. There will be no tribunal or trial to decide if I'm worthy of Heaven. The sooner we dispel with these manmade fantasies and realize they were stories our parents told us to keep us in line, the better off we will be. When we die, we return to our source. Call it Heaven, Paradise, Nirvana, Valhalla, it doesn't matter. It's all the same place, in the same way there is only one God.

We get so caught up in naming of things, making up stories and constructs to explain how things are and how things are going to be, that we forget the most important thing, and that is love. God is love. Heaven is a place of love. So, quite simply - BE LOVE. We spend too much time thinking and less being. If we were to be love now, Heaven would be available to us right here, right now. Personally, I don't even care if my vision of Heaven is wrong. When I die and finally see it for what it is, I'm just going to say, "Oh, so this is how it works!" I'm not going to worry about it, because right here and now I'm going to live my life as if Heaven were open to me right here and now. I'm going to love and love and love. I'm not afraid of dying, because I'm too busy living. I live with infinite possibilities, because with God, anything is possible. Infinity is limitless and has no boundaries. While I'm here I intend to live the same way, and when I do move on I am going to just keep on keeping on.

As I've said over and over, it's all about love. That is the true nature of your infinite self, so be that self and nothing else. Let that spirit guide you day by day. Not all days are going to be good, but more often than not, you'll find that if you lead with love, that will be a good day too.

Now, just imagine if we could all do this and all be on the same page at the same time. Wouldn't that be amazing?

Chapter 7 - Universal Cooperation

Survival of the Friendliest

Ever since I was young I was taught the value of competition. Competing strengths, physical traits, ideas, values, and strategies are pitted against one another, and through the process of natural selection, only the best attributes, ideas, strengths and strategies win. Competition assures that only the best reach the peak, and everyone benefits from the cream rising to the top. There must be winners and losers to assure gene pools are not weakened, thus preventing a species from going extinct. Cultures benefit and grow, because new and better ideas are always challenging the status quo. Consumers benefit because competition in business assures that only the best products succeed in the marketplace.

There is a lot of merit in these concepts. For instance, the idea that only giraffes with long necks survived, because only they were the only ones who could reach the food in the trees, makes sense to me. The strongest bull mates with the cows. I get that. And most certainly, sporting events would be much less fun if athletes didn't compete. However, we tend to fixate on competition to a point of obsession that leads to a skewed sense of social values. We feel a need to dominate things, dominate people, be the dominant species or dominant religion. We perceive differences between ourselves and the "other." Once we objectify things as different from ourselves, we lose sight of our connectedness. We begin to forget our connection to all things and see ourselves as separate from them. Once we create this separation, the unity that is the common chord of our natural state of being is weakened, and we can't reach our true potential.

What if, just WHAT IF, we put more emphasis on helping one another instead of being in competition with one another? Synergy? Unity? Cooperation? That sounds so much better than "domination." The reality is that we achieve more through cooperation than competition, and if you look at the natural world, there's evidence of this. Even though there is competition among species in nature, their survival is based on cooperation.

Let's use tech terms as a model. Think of a world filled with different species of microchips, processors, modules, apps, and programs, each functioning interdependently to sustain a healthy ecosystem, or in this case a properly functioning computer. Each species competes for resources and energy, all the while coexisting for a common cause. A malfunction in the system occurs when there is conflict between competing programs or hardware, or when one of the components breaks or gets removed. So too, this occurs in the natural world.

The Wolves of Yellowstone

One of the best examples of cooperation in nature is the reintroduction of wolves into Yellowstone National Park and the fascinating results that came from that program.

Wolves had been absent in Yellowstone since the early 1900's. They were thought to be a threat to people and livestock and were all but exterminated from America's lower 48 states. When they were reintroduced into Yellowstone in 1995, wolves flourished. Then people began to notice something interesting with ecology of Yellowstone's ecosystem.

For a long time, beavers and other animals were almost completely absent from certain areas of Yellowstone, and nobody could figure out why. Elk populations enjoyed life without one of its top predators to bother them. As a result elk herds overpopulated the lush lowlands and valleys, eating young willow tree seedlings and other vegetation near rivers and streams. These plants are important in preventing erosion along the banks of rivers, because their roots help to hold the soil in place.

Over time, these elk populations began to change the ecology of Yellowstone and the ecosystem began to suffer, forcing many species of birds and mammals to relocate. When wolves were reintroduced, elk numbers began to decrease as their herds were hunted and forced back up into high lands. This allowed Yellowstone's alluvial lands to return to something closer to their original, pre-1900 condition. Plant life started to flourish again and stabilization of riverbanks even caused some streams and rivers to change course. Animals like the beaver and bears eventually returned after being gone from these areas for nearly 100 years. With the return of the wolf, all of the components that work together to form a healthy ecosystem in Yellowstone were once again in place.

This story is not just an example of how removing one species can change an entire ecosystem, it also shows us how species interact and coexist to define a *healthy* ecosystem. It shows the interdependence of plants and animals, working together and doing what they do naturally. Nothing is forced. Nothing is deliberate. There are no egos involved. The wolf is being a wolf. The willow is being a willow, and the beaver is being a beaver. As human beings, our reach and ability to modify our environment is enormous, making us just as much a part of the Yellowstone ecosystem as the wolf. When we removed the wolf from that ecosystem, we contributed to the breakdown of its natural processes – and we must take responsibility for creating that breakdown.

When we reintroduced the wolf back into Yellowstone National Park, we humans grew as a species. We learned we could live in concert with wolves, respecting their place amidst the order of all species.

Fear and naiveté caused us to make a bad decision and attempt to annihilate an entire species. Wisdom and compassion allowed us to make up for our mistake. Sadly, we will continue to make these mistakes until we learn to live in peace with all things and all people.

It Takes a Village

In the United States, as with many parts of the world, there is an incredible homeless problem. People have been forced from their homes due to poor economic conditions or because they suffer from mental illness or drug addiction or some combination of all the above. They are seen as the outcasts of society, attracting more scorn than compassion from people of means. Many people tend to look away rather than look to help, and that is a prime example of the skewed ideals that our competitive society creates. Nobody likes a loser, so we turn a blind eye.

Many children today are never given a chance to know what it's like to be part of a loving family, and are orphaned or thrust into a foster care system that is broken. Without the love of parents and family, these children are raised in a cold, unforgiving world, often with very few options other than finding support from street gangs and a life of crime.

Without family as the primary source of love and wellbeing, it really does take a village to raise a child nowadays. If we are to change the course of these children's futures, we not only need to provide them with opportunities, we also need to show them a world where they are loved and can be guided to these opportunities by people who care enough to show them the way. They need to be assured that they are not alone. The ideals of "community" must be engendered to future generations if we are to stem the tide of apathy that drives the chronic problems we face in our communities today.

One of the cornerstones of community is cooperation. Community is neighbors working together to make their little slice of the world a better place. As our population increases, the need for community also increases, as we find more and more people living in close proximity to one another. We want to feel safe in our communities. We want our kids to be safe when they go outside. We want to know that someone is watching out for us.

Several years ago, there was a massive power outage in my neighborhood due to heavy rains. For three days, most of the town was without power. It was a curious sight to see orange extension cords extending through yards, from one house to another, as neighbors with generators helped fellow neighbors keep freezers running so that food wouldn't spoil. Groups of neighbors went from house to house to help pump water out of their neighbors' basements. Nobody thought about it. They just acted. That kind of cooperative effort is the essence of community.

Resistance in Society

Think of all the problems in the world today that are based on an us-versus-them mentality that competition creates. You've heard me talk about resistance in previous chapters: anytime something pushes against something else, resistance is created. Like a brake rubbing against a wheel to slow it from spinning, we create resistance in our world that slows our growth. We spend more time on conflict resolution than we do on solving the problems that would allow us to grow as a global community!

War is generating a worldwide refugee problem, leaving people without a home or country. People continue to go hungry in third-world nations. Many don't have access to clean drinking water. Yet, we find it far more important to debate over whether we should build walls around our country to keep these people out. The wealthiest nations in the world have the capacity to eliminate hunger everywhere, yet they waste billions of dollars defending what is theirs by playing a global chess match to increase their stockpiles. Corporations move their manufacturing to deprived regions of the world and pay people pennies on the dollar, not because they want to bring opportunity to these people, but because the move increases the company's bottom line.

All of these scenarios are based on the mindset that the good of the few outweighs the good of the many. This mentality is so deeply seated into our society that it has become the norm, and we have trouble imagining it any other way. Human beings have been in conflict like this ever since rival families of cavemen found it easier to take the land and resources of another family instead of cooperating and sharing the land. This behavioral theme can be found among other species in nature as well. Chimpanzees and apes also form troops that fight among themselves. Most predatory species like wolves, bears, and lions fight over territorial boundaries. But one thing separates us from these animals, and that is our ability to reason and exercise compassion.

Imagine a world where everyone got along, nobody went to bed hungry, and nobody lacked anything they needed to survive. It is in the realm of human capacity to create such a society, and has long been discussed by many of history's greatest scholars. Yet, we continue to resist the idea like the plague. This resistance may have worked fine up until now, but the human species is reaching its tipping point.

There are currently around seven billion of us humans and counting, each of us needing food, fresh water, and room to move. We reached our first billion inhabitants on this planet in the late 1800's. By the time I was born in 1966, we numbered between three and four billion. In just 50 short years, that number has doubled again, and continues to grow exponentially. "Exponentially" means that the human population is not growing at a steady rate anymore. It now continues to pick up speed, growing faster and faster.

This growth will not subside until a disaster like world famine or a world war drastically reduces our numbers. Sadly, in our current state, one of those scenarios is almost inevitable unless we learn to get along. Our planet is a limited resource, meaning there is a limit to how many people Earth can sustain before our population begins to decrease due to a lack of resources. We are at a pivotal moment in our evolution, where we must decide the best course of action before the proverbial speeding car we're in slams into the wall that's fast approaching.

"Carrying Capacity" is the term used to describe the number of people the world can sustain based on available resources of fresh water, food, and other factors. According to the United Nations Environmental Programme's June 2012 report, the majority of studies conducted point to our reaching carrying capacity at or around eight billion people by the year 2027. The next largest group of studies is more optimistic, believing our carrying capacity will be around 16 billion people, or about twice the size of our current population.

Any way you look at it, we are growing faster and faster with more and more mouths to feed. But instead of working together for the common good, we still fight and scheme to hoard resources at the expense of others. Let's ask the big question: What would our true Nature of Being tell us to do?

I wouldn't call myself a socialist, because I do not believe it's a government's job to take complete care of its people. However, I do believe that people should take care of people. And I'm referring to all people, no matter where they are on this planet. We possess the consciousness and compassion to know and do what's right. We need to get past all ideological differences that create the resistance that is slowing our mental and spiritual growth, especially while population growth increases unimpeded.

It comes down to the choices of how we govern ourselves and how we choose to define ourselves as *people*. Look at the thousands of years of history where humans have lived in society. Where has conflict and competition gotten us? Some societies still believe that life is cheap. There is inequality because of the perception of inequality. We continue to believe we are not all one in the eyes of God. Compassion has taken a backseat to the endless pursuit of more stuff, which creates endless disparity among people. At what point do we draw the line and say enough is enough? I know what's right, and I believe you do too. When will the true leaders of this world unify us for the common good of all? When will we realize we're inevitably going to reach a point where people are going to die simply because there is no longer enough to go around?

Time is ticking on the human experience. In a thousand years from now, we will have either reached utopia through our efforts or removed ourselves from this planet completely. The Earth will not sustain us in our current state, although it will continue through the millennia quite well without us. We impact the Earth more than any other species, and we have the ability to choose what that effect will be. Why not imagine a world without hunger, a world in peace where nobody is in need of anything? If we conceive it and believe it, anything is possible. We simply create our own resistance by saying it's not possible.

Welcoming Universal Cooperation

If cooperation is the key to our success, then compassion towards one another is its motivation. Looking beyond our fear-based society, and taking a leap of faith in believing that all people are good and capable of great love, is the most important step we all need to take. Cooperation on a global scale may seem like a flight of fancy, but that's because we only think of it in terms of our current conditions and past experiences.

What if we all pretend for a minute that we don't have the answer? Instead, let go of the fear and let love guide you. Liberate yourself from the need to acquire more stuff and begin thinking in terms of what is better for all. Picture what we could do if we no longer needed to focus on building walls to protect what is mine or yours, and could direct that attention to more productive things. We would be free to allow for greater beauty in the world, solve problems, grow in intellect, create beautiful works of art, and expand our minds to new heights. That's what it will take for us to begin creating as God creates. That is what we are intended to do here on Earth. That is why we are here.

Just think of the potential of seven billion people creating as God intended and what that would be like. I envision a world where all problems can be overcome, a world where people work together toward common goals that benefit all people. A world where no one lacks anything they need to survive. A world finally at peace. These ideas only seem farfetched because we're used to focusing on what is not possible and talk ourselves out of what is possible. If only we believed it could be. I choose to believe it not only could be, but must be. There is no other way without adding more loss and suffering to the equation. How can we be satisfied with anything short of universal cooperation if the end result is peace?

Still, none of this can happen until we release the fear that keeps telling us that none of this is possible. We need to start trusting one another. And for us to trust one another, we need to each be accountable for ourselves. We need to be accountable for our actions and our beliefs. We need to be able to admit when we're wrong. We need to stop blowing each other up. We need to stop being afraid.

Finally, we need to understand our place here on Earth. We play a huge role in the web of life. Historically, we have viewed ourselves as a higher being separate from all other living things, when in reality we are intricately connected to them. Universal cooperation extends beyond human interactions, putting us squarely in the middle of the natural world. Like the wolf, the willow, the elk and the beaver, the world would be a different place without us.

So here we are, seven billion strong and growing. How will we choose to live our lives from here on out? As our numbers continue to grow, we need to work together and be even more vigilant, to cooperate and live in peace with each other. Our future as a species depends on it. Will we continue to believe we have dominion over nature, or will we accept our role as stewards of the Earth? Will we choose to work together and advance to a higher consciousness, or will we continue on our current path and never achieve our true potential? It will come down to our choices. Only time will tell.

Chapter 8 - Return to Nature

I Walk the Woods of My Childhood

I begin my walk in the woods down by the Des Plaines River, entering the forest through an alluvial plain. The soil is moist from frequent flooding. Here I find silver maples, ash and swamp white oaks flourishing. As I ascend the plain away from the river, I rise up to find sugar maples and white oaks. As I get higher above the plain, the forest changes to black cherries and red oaks. Each one of these trees is perfectly suited for the climate, moisture, and soil conditions it grows in. Each has its purpose in the intricate web of its habitat. Their connection to all things results in a patchwork of diversity that extends through all the species present. It is a connection through all things that we too are connected to and a part of.

I have been walking these same paths through the woods since I was a teen. In my youth, I was quite a hiker, backpacking in Yellowstone, Glacier National Park, and Isle Royale, among other places. I use to pride myself at the distances I could walk in a day. As I grew older, my pace got slower. The distance travelled got shorter, not because of my age or my health, but because I began to notice more things along my path. I wasn't as concerned with traveling a certain distance in a day and instead began finding more enjoyment in what I found along the way. In the haste of my youth, I had passed up so many of the wonders of nature that lay before me. I cannot begin to imagine the things I missed! Once I began to slow down and stop all together at times, I began to notice what was at my feet - patterns in nature, cause-and-effect events and anomalies I could not explain. The ensuing fascination captivated me and made me question how ecosystems and the natural world function as a whole.

My hunger for knowledge compelled me to learn all I could know about the world around me. I wanted to learn what every plant was, why it grew where it grew, and what animals were best suited for the habitat provided. I wanted to know about climates and weather patterns and how they affected the land. I dug into the soil and saw the history of the Earth unfold. I could now see the forest for the trees in a way most people could not. The more I noticed, the more I understood the intricate workings of life on our planet.

I began to feel a familiar kinship to nature I had never realized. It is one I had long felt, but never understood completely. I began to see how I was part of this amazing dance we all perform in nature, how species interact and affect each other, and how my actions have their effect on the rest of the world. This gave me a sense of belonging. To recognize that I am part of nature helped me to appreciate my connection to all creation and how we all come from the same creative source. The unity and oneness of our spirit connects all things. There is no higher order of being. Creation is equal in every measure.

It's a humbling experience when you realize your own fragility, that you have no dominion over anything and that everything has just as much right to exist as you do. That epiphany alone has helped me understand how to love absolutely.

Adopt the Pace of Nature

Through nature, I learned the value of patience. I saw how slow nature's pace can be, the infinite patience of change, and how it could benefit my life if I too adopted that pace. It takes millions of years of tectonic activity for the Earth's crust to heave upward to form mountains, and millions of years for a river to carve out a valley. If you want to move mountains, stop trying to force it and let nature take its course.

That attitude has paid dividends for my own peace of mind. Perhaps the greatest wisdom we can learn from nature is that nothing ever happens exactly when or how we want it to. And, when things seem to go your way, it's fleeting because one of the constants in nature is change. Knowing this has allowed me to approach life with much greater fluidity. One of my favorite sayings is, *If you want to make God laugh, just tell him your plans.* With that in mind, whenever I set a goal for myself, I always leave plenty of room for course corrections and improvisation.

The only time nature doesn't move slowly is when there is a cataclysmic event. The meteor that killed off the dinosaurs and other major extinction events during Earth's history created almost immediate change to the natural world. Genetic mutations have created whole new species seemingly overnight. However, when you consider the age of the Earth in billions of years, these seemingly instantaneous events may actually have taken thousands if not millions of years to happen.

In life, you may have a need for quick or sudden change. If something in your life isn't working, by all means change it. Choosing to write this book was a drastic change for me. I never imagined I would write a book until one day the idea grew in me, and it grew and grew until one day I was ready and simply started writing. This all seemed to happen suddenly once the idea of writing a book broke its bonds and my thoughts began to unfold on these pages. But remember, it's been nearly 30 years since the initial seed began to germinate in me, when my younger self picked up that yellow legal pad and began to write. For me, nature took its course and continues to do so as I sit here writing today. Wisdom comes with time. I've become wiser in my actions, choosing to think things through, reacting less, and learning to take advantage of more opportunities as they come my way. Animals in their natural habitat are the ultimate opportunists. Their survival depends upon a calculated expenditure of energy, so animals do not waste energy if they don't need to. A predator rarely chases its prey, for example, instead relying more on ambush tactics that require only short bursts of energy.

I too have learned not to chase. In the past, I spent a lot of energy on things that I needed to let go of. I knew I had to close the doors of my first business long before I ever did, refusing to accept that it was failing. I chose to endure needless hardship over cutting my losses and moving on. Recently, I noticed I have a tendency to hang on to negative feelings longer than I should. When I get angry, I dwell on that anger, taking time and energy away from more productive activities. If I imagine myself in the role of a predator that needs to conserve this energy, I can see how my tendency to not let go is hindering me. Take a moment to imagine yourself as a predator. What are some things you might be doing in your life that cause you to waste energy?

Prey animals have developed heightened senses that allow them to be more aware of potential dangers around them. In fact, animals like deer usually know you are nearby before you are even aware of them. They first size you up and evaluate the level of danger. If you get too close, they flee just far and fast enough to mitigate the danger while always conserving their energy for when it's needed. These animals not only know how to conserve energy, they have made awareness of danger their number one priority. By putting yourself in the role of a prey animal, see if you can identify any habits or tendencies that you might have adopted that prevent you from avoiding danger.

Through nature, there is a lot we can learn about ourselves. Fear and worry have been the greatest energy drainers of my wellbeing. Instead of giving in to fear and worry, I've learned to rely more on awareness and intuition, taking advantage of opportunities, and conserving energy. I've learned to take my time, pace myself, and know all the risks and rewards before I take action.

The Animal Within

Mindful of my thoughts and actions, I've taken cues from animals, both predator and prey, to govern myself more effectively through life. There is a lot we can learn from nature when we observe and pay attention. Understanding that I am part of nature has allowed me to see these cues more clearly and adapt my life to them.

We are not so far removed from other predator or prey species in this world. Our natural instincts have become softened by behaviors we have adopted when we began to see ourselves as separate from all other things. We've gotten lost in our humanness. Our need to hunt and forage only goes as far as a trip to the grocery store now. We've adopted habits that are counterproductive to natural instincts that lay dormant in our psyche. We are safe within our four walls, and our need for survival has been replaced by a need for more stuff, bigger homes, bigger TVs, and other things that feed our egos. We see ourselves as separate and different, and that has opened a Pandora's box to a host of deviant values and behaviors.

Maligned values can become perverted to a point that we begin to lose respect for life in general. The senseless taking of life, and the cruelty we exhibit toward each other and other species, is just not acceptable in my mind. We are the only species capable of true evil. All other species on this planet live instinctively, acting within their true nature. A predator is simply being a predator. Even though nature can seem cruel at times, other animals don't shoot up movie theaters and schools for no apparent reason. They do not kill over political or religious views.

It is important to remind myself of the animal within me. Just below the surface of my consciousness is the instinctive animal that I am. These instincts, which function as a means for me to survive, are part of my true nature. By understanding this instinctive side of my nature and how it affects my ability to reason, I solidify my connection to nature, all things, and all people. I can choose to be good or evil. I can choose to be more like God and create as God creates, always knowing that underneath is an animal whose function is to survive.

This survival instinct is incredibly powerful, and most times people don't even realize it. The fight or flight instinct is biologically innate. People tend to do things they wouldn't do under normal circumstances, especially in times of panic. People getting trampled by a fleeing crowd is an extreme example of this. Nobody in the crowd is intentionally killing or harming another person. They are merely reacting in panic, and their survival instinct is so strong that their ability to reason has gone out the window. They are just doing whatever it takes to survive.

Understanding the choice between good and evil is an easy one, yet human beings still make poor choices that harm others. Does this make them evil, or are they reacting to a fight-or-flight situation they find themselves in? The world is full of reactionary choices that people make without consciously evaluating long-term outcomes and effects. Reactive people are often the detractors in life that add so much resistance to the experience of other folks who are just trying to get along. Selfishness itself is not evil, but it does lie at the root of most problems that create this resistance. With a little exercise in mindfulness, much of this resistance can be avoided.

When you get inside your head and complicate things, you create your own problems. When you attune your life to the pace of nature, and exist more instinctually within the realm of your true nature, you remove the clutter that is in your way. When you get down to what is more instinctive - that which originates from your loving self - you can begin to ask yourself, "What feels right? What is the right thing to do?" The connection to your natural self gets bridged across the shortest distance possible.

Living by instinct strips away your dependence on conscious thought. This allows your animal nature to focus on only your basic needs, removing all superfluous desires. When you do let conscious thought back in, you can choose the thoughts you focus upon. This allows you to be more singularly focused on your true nature. It's like hitting the consciousness reset button, clearing out the junk and allowing only the thoughts that serve you.

We are not and need not be far removed from our animal self. Our instinctive being is part of the purest form of ourselves. In nature, animals and plants live their life's purpose simply by being as they were intended. Plants grow and compete for sunlight. All the while they take in CO_2 and create life-sustaining oxygen. All animals live and die fulfilling their niche in their ecosystem, oblivious to the role they play in it. As conscious human beings, we too can live instinctively, living as we are intended to be.

The next time you find yourself making what might be a poor choice, ask yourself how much of that choice is based on your instinct to survive. The right choice may not be the popular one. You may need to seriously weigh the consequences of your actions, looking at the benefit compared to the detriment to you and others. Before you make any choice that could impose harm, be it on people, animals, plants, or the planet itself, say to yourself, *I am one with God and one with all things in nature. This is where I choose to reside.* Then make the choice that is in greatest alignment with that affirmation.

Your Return to Nature

What is it about going outside and being in nature that changes us, revives us, and heals us? It's more than just fresh air, though I believe that is a big part of it. Nobody goes on vacation and stays indoors, unless you're on your honeymoon or it's raining cats and dogs. No, we go outside. We put our toes in the sand. We hike. We swim. We ski. We go outside to feel the warm sun on our face. I think the sun gets a bad rap. We live most of our lives indoors, and when we do go outside, we're told we need to cover up? We need the sun. It fuels us. It's the most natural source of vitamin D there is, unless you're eating tons of certain types of fatty fish or beef liver.

But there's another aspect of returning to nature that is of a more spiritual nature. It is the idea that we need to be more firmly planted on the Earth. We need to feel the Earth under our feet. We need to physically touch nature to gain the sense of our connectedness to it. All things in life are energy, whether they are living or not. I believe the Earth is alive in a sense we do not understand. We do not know how a tree thinks, yet it too is alive all the same. How often do you feel the ground beneath your feet? I love walking barefoot in the grass. It's the only time I feel completely connected to the Earth.

Apart from the beneficial exercise, a walk in nature also brings you closer to your natural self. People who live in urban environments need to find a patch of green and walk in it. It's also important for cities to promote green spaces. We've become disjointed in large urban areas due to the lack of any oases of trees, grass, and plants. Only people who take the time or have the resources to travel out to the country get to benefit from a walk in the woods, so we need to bring nature to people.

By incorporating green spaces into an urban environment, we create a patchwork of natural areas that join larger natural areas together. Instead of having large urban islands that are devoid of nature, our cities become more incorporated into our natural surroundings. This is not only beneficial to people living in the cities, but it is incredibly helpful to wildlife that need natural land bridges for migration that are otherwise cut off by urban development. Many cities that have adopted this initiative have experienced an influx of wildlife that was never there before. The natural balance of nature is being restored, not to mention improved air quality and happier residents.

Experiencing nature in our lives is essential to our wellbeing. If you're feeling blue, go take a walk. It sounds so cliché, but it's the truth. A walk outside will do you wonders. We need to feel our connectedness to the Earth because we are part of it, and that connection is so important to who we are. The lessons we learn from our first and only home are the guide to living a more fulfilling life.

Put the pieces together. Every aspect of your true nature can be found in nature. Respect for all life, balance and connectedness, all are part of your natural self and the natural world around you. Love comes easily when you understand your connection to all things. Life becomes easy when love is the absolute essence of who you are. Joy. Happiness. Contentment. Peace of mind. They are all byproducts of a life filled with absolute love.

When you embrace your love for all things and seek to understand your connection to it all, you discover your true self.

Chapter 9 - Being a Creator

What is God's Intention?

God is love. If God intends us to create, then that is our purpose. We are creators of God's love. It was said to me recently by someone who had read my work that they could tell I love God very much. I smiled and said, "I am simply being as God intends me to be." I love all things and all people very much, so it only stands to reason that I love God very much. God needs no praise, no worship, only a conscious deliberate effort to be like God. If God is love - then love! You don't seek love, so don't attempt to find love. Love is God, so be love! You have the power to be as God intends simply by being as God intends. It's already within you. It was the one gift given to you when you were conceived and born into this world. Our consciousness creates problems that blur the vision of our true intention. It now lies as a latent memory within you, waiting to be rediscovered.

When you finally rediscover this intention and arrive at the "ah-ha" moment, you begin to become *God-realized*. God realization happens when you finally put all the pieces together and understand there is no separation between you, God, or everything and everyone else. You begin to let go of old beliefs that have kept you trapped. The walls that created division and separation crumble, and love flows freely from you. It is an amazing sense of freedom and liberation when you discover that everything you've been searching for has been right inside of you all along. When you no longer allow doubt and fear to guide you and distort your perception, you begin to see the truth.

It can be a slow process. It didn't happen overnight for me, and I continue to learn and practice every day. For me, I've needed to cut through more than 40 years of bad habits, misguided ideas, and confusion to get to the truth about who I really am. The younger you are when you make this leap, the better off you'll be. After years and years of being told who my enemies are and who not to trust, I can now look back and see how far I've come. But I often wonder how different my life would have been had I not been taught those false beliefs in the first place. That is the goal of future generations: freedom to know who you truly are from day one.

When you achieve God realization, you begin to see the world for what it is. You have no enemies. Instead, you recognize how so many people are out of alignment and how much work really needs to be done to shift the consciousness of the world to what God intends for us. That's why taking the next step past *realization* is so important.

Once you are God-realized, it only takes a simple step to become *God-actualized*. God actualization is when you begin to live your life as God intends. You begin to use the gifts that were bestowed upon you to achieve a very specific purpose. Chances are you're already using those talents in some form or another. The only difference is now you must begin to use them with love as your intention. Instead of money, power, or fame as your motivation, you begin to think about doing what's right for the world. You add to the collective consciousness of God's intention. That is why we're here. When we all become God-actualized, we are not only functioning as God intended, we've also become the physical manifestation of God's truth and the love that God is.

I envision a day when children are born into a world that is free of confusion. There will be no relearning to change bad habits or misguided thoughts. The God realization we know at birth will be actualized by our parents and doctors and everyone we encounter in life. I once believed that this was the endgame for us and the ultimate goal of our species, resulting in our ascension to Heaven. But I now believe that this will only be the end of a particular chapter in our existence. After all, life is a journey, so why would it need to end there? My mind now begs to imagine what the future of human beings will be once God actualization is achieved by all.

The Purpose of Ego

Psychiatrist Carl Jung suggested that as an acorn becomes an oak tree, so too human beings should become what they are meant to be. But most of us find ourselves stuck, and this is because we don't give an appropriate amount of time looking inward to understand the duality of our being. We tend to externalize and stay consciously one-sided.

Looking at both halves of our self - our ego-self and our natural-self - there needs to be a balance that we achieve and maintain. Don't try to turn off the ego. Just understand it for what it is and keep it in balance with the person you are meant to be. Allow the ego to help propel your reality while keeping one foot firmly planted in the foundation of your natural-self, who you are meant to be, and who you are constantly becoming.

When your ego is in front of you, it's easier to keep watch over it. It can't escape you or take over, because you are constantly aware of it. Let your ego create the motion that manifests the things you want and need in your life - while you are formulating your beliefs and making decisions based on your natural self. This way, you are aware of the duality and in control of both sides. If you allow your ego to be in control, you would never understand that duality, because the ego does not like to share the spotlight.

However, do not confuse your duality with the cliché of the angel and devil sitting on your shoulders. When you exist from your natural-self, there is no devil to encourage you to do the wrong thing. Your ego is not the devil, but it can lead you in the wrong direction if you let it. From the viewpoint of your natural-self however, there is clarity. It's all right in front of you. You face choices and understand right and wrong. Your moral compass allows you to navigate and decide when your ego should assert itself.

Ego has its purpose. It gives you your individuality. It enables you to assert your ideas and creativity out into the world. You have the ability to conceive of things that no one else has thought of until you came around. Simply put, if we didn't have egos, we would lack individuality and all be the same.

I can firmly say that I am not the same person I was in my youth. I'm not even the same person I was last year, last month or last week. What I had believed in then, I may not believe today, and what I believe today may change again tomorrow. We are constantly being given new data that adjusts our perception of the world around us, and the ego is more than happy to adjust our mood to this changing information. When I was young, I would react more often, flying off the handle at times. My ego was in control. I was in the process of defining myself, and when the world would push me, I pushed back. Now, I'm more inclined to remain balanced toward things that don't affect me directly, and I choose my battles wisely. Every new piece of information is a chance to learn and grow. As I learn more about myself, I realize there is less for me to defend.

As we age, our ego no longer serves us as it did when we were younger. There becomes less of a need to define our individuality. Our values change from taking care of ourselves to taking care of our children and our aging parents. Kicking and screaming, we let go of our ego-self and enter parenthood and middle age. Many people experience a shift in consciousness and values at this time. The ego's role diminishes and gets placed in permanent check, often accompanied by a spiritual awakening. This is also a time when some of us get stuck. The ego does not go down without a fight! It's the classic midlife crisis, earmarked by narcissism, selfish acts, and poor choices.

Regardless of your age, what matters is that you exist from your natural-self and be the person you are meant to be. Take the high road and follow your moral compass. Allow your ego to define your individuality, because that's the outward part of you that everybody sees first. That's the fun side of you. The caring mother, the loyal friend, the big brother, the father figure, the coach, the teacher, and all the characteristics that make 'you' who you are, these are the lasting impressions you leave in the perceptions of others when the ego works in concert with your natural-self.

This character, portrayed by you, is brought to life by your ego. There's only a problem when ego escapes the watchful eye of your natural-self and begins calling the shots. The caring mother becomes the boastful parent, telling everyone what a great job she does. The coach is no longer humble about accepting accolades. The charitable person gets hooked on posting messages of their good deeds for people to see on social media. All are functions of an ego going too far and saying "Look at me."

All that you need to do is to keep the ego in its place. Your natural-self must ultimately steer the ship to keep your life on course. After all, the ego as we know it is not going to go away anytime soon. It's just as much part of you and me as our appendix and opposable thumbs. Time and evolution will decide its fate. For now, embrace the ego as part of you and always exist from your natural-self.

Your Creative Connection

The best way to avoid the pitfalls of the ego is to maintain your constant connection with the creative source of all things. Remember you are part of the eternal matrix of God's universe and your soul too is eternal. For me, it's much less about remembering than knowing. It's something that in and of itself is an eternal thought. It is being who you are. Knowing your physical existence is merely a projection of your infinite self. You are timeless by nature and created for an instant of infinity in goodness and love.

Your day-to-day actions will ultimately be in alignment with your true nature when you exist from this constant sense of knowing. As a result, your ego never has an opportunity to take control. It will constantly try, however. It will attempt to instill doubt. Recognize that fear is ego's attack on you, a way of trying to deride your virtue. Your ego can be your own worst enemy. By maintaining your eternal connection with your natural-self, you begin to see ego for exactly what it is.

You are meant to create as God intends you to create. The paradox of the ego manifests in your conscious choices between good and bad, right and wrong. If the ego were removed, there would be only one good, right choice. And if that were the case, there would be no consciousness, only instinct. The paradox goes further when you consider that the choice to create or destroy is one and the same. After all, when you destroy something you are actually creating something else. We always talk about the destructive force of volcanoes, earthquakes, and tsunamis. They're considered natural disasters. A disaster is a bad thing. When there is a disaster, there is loss. However, these natural events are also part of a creative process that builds mountains, realigns tectonic plates, and constantly modifies and creates only as nature knows how.

In the realm of human creation however, there is a constant unifying theme to what we create. We are meant to learn from our creations. We learn about our connectedness. We learn about love and how we are all meant to unify our connectedness with love. These are our lessons of eternity and why we keep going around and around until we get it right. Purgatory, if there is such a thing, is like after-school detention. Our ultimate creation is to be released from the cycle of learning and unlearning until we are creating as we are meant to create. When the ego is allowed to run amuck, it creates and destroys to satisfy only for personal gains, and that is a real recipe for disaster.

It all comes back to love. Is there love in what you do? Is love the reason you do what you do? If so, you are creating as God creates. Your connection is complete. You can now begin the process of going from student to teacher, leading by your example. Teach those around you about love by *being* love. Teach those around you about the ego by being selfless. Teach those around you about God by creating as God intends you to create. Throw in a little compassion, joy, patience, and trust for good measure, and you will be the light for all to see. Open yourself to others as you open yourself to God, for they are one in the same. This is your creative connection. This is your purpose for being.

There are no accidents in life. One lesson is learned, leading to the next lesson. We stumble and fumble through life never achieving balance, because our ego gives us a misguided perception of what it is that we want and need. Let go and let God guide you toward becoming what you already are at the core of your existence. You are a perfect piece of the infinite, creative source that created you. Be that infinite creative source you are already are. Become what is divinely intended for you by understanding your duality and your ability to choose between what is wrong and right, and only doing what is right. Take the high road and do what you do with all the love that is eternally woven into the fibers of your soul.

Begin by being a creator in your life. Find purpose in what you do. Do this and change the world for the better. Do this and you will have accomplished your creative connection with an infinite source of possibilities. Do this and you will fulfill all your needs and desires, because you have unlocked the door to an infinite source of possibilities. As you do, an interesting thing will happen along the way. You will discover the true potential of your being.

Chapter 10 - Becoming the Change

Now that you have a better idea of what your natural-self is and how it operates from love, you can begin your journey inward to discover your true self. In the next section of the book, I want to share with you things I have learned that have helped me along the way. But before I do, I want to close this section by sharing why we need to take this journey.

I never thought I would find myself among generations of people who live at such a pivotal time in human history. We've certainly had doomsayers throughout history, and many close calls. We've had predictions and prophecies and a tangled web of conspiracy theories that have made us all a bit immune to what we see with our own eyes. The opposite of love is not hate. It is apathy. The world has gone to sleep. I'm not predicting the end of days. What I am seeing is just more of the same, only on a grander scale.

Historically, we have muddled through generations, progressing fractionally based on our human needs, but more or less repeating the same mistakes over and over again. We have proven to be more clever than wise, always fixing problems but not preventing them from happening.

Lessons of the past are repeated continually. Only now, as the world becomes more crowded, these lessons when repeated seem to have much greater impact. At what point do we realize that we are all in this together?

We all have such an amazing opportunity to do great things. Each and every one of us has been given a gift - our divine inheritance, our special purpose. What we do with that gift is up to us to share. Many take that gift to the grave with them, never expressing their true purpose. Some are taken from this life before they have a chance to express it. There are millions of people starving and suffering needlessly. So many people die in wars they do not want. Is it insane to want peace? I think not. So, why isn't it considered insane to want war? What are we defending? What is there to protect that is worth dying for other than life itself? An ideal? A need to be right?

Sure, if you are attacked, you should defend yourself and protect the life you've been given. But, the error in our ways is in the attack. Too many people hold their ego up like a shield, creating false honor while duped by pseudo-patriotism and propaganda. Love for love's sake takes a backseat to love of country and devotion to religion. When this happens, we open ourselves to manipulation. We are no longer thinking for ourselves. That is how a leader like Adolph Hitler seduced a country into murdering six million Jews and fanned the flames of a world war that took the lives of 60 million people.

Think about that for a moment. In the six years of World War II, 60 million souls were denied their chance for greatness. When I say *greatness*, I refer to their ability to love and to learn and teach others about love. We all talk about peace. We pray for peace and greet each other with words like "Peace be with you." But, who among us is willing to set aside our differences and create peace that holds no attachments or conditions? Our world leaders pride themselves as peacekeepers, signing treaties weighed down by conditions and stipulations. They divide up lands, create borders, and build walls. These peace treaties are doomed to fail, because eventually the lines will be broken and borders will be crossed. There can be no lasting peace without a treaty that is created for the sake of peace alone.

Today, there are more than seven billion of us crowding this planet. How many of us are going to choose to be the light? How many of us are going to break from our historic mindset and change the way we think about ourselves and each other? If we continue to think in terms of what is mine and what is yours, we are guaranteed to see a greater escalation in tension all around. Think of it like a rush-hour train car that continues to fill up at every stop. As more people enter, the more crowded it becomes. As more people get on, bodies are forced closer and closer together. We can choose kindness and let people into our personal space, or we can let our discomfort get the best of us and start pushing people away.

It is the ability to let go and let others in that allows us to lose that uncomfortable feeling. We can't change the situation at this point. The train is going to continue to pick up more people. Accept that you can't have the world to yourself, and try to appreciate the person next to you and your divine connection to them. See yourself in them and surrender the judgment of your differences. Once you let them in, love begins to flow freely and without conditions.

The experience of letting people in is an energy onto itself. When you give that energy away to those around you, tensions naturally subside. That's the power of a smile. The gentleness and sincerity you share tells others that it's okay to do the same. It's a natural progression based on the fact that everyone, at the core of their being, wants the same thing. We all want peace for the sake of peace. That is the unifying goal of our natural-self. That is the essence of our divinity. The gifts we are given at birth are meant to foster this goal. It is the recognition of our divinity that allows us to get out of our own way and to stop being selfish.

The world does not revolve around me. Nor should you think it revolves around you. We are all in this crazy, wonderful life together, and it is what we make of it. If we can ever get past out differences and break down the walls that separate us, we will all be in a better place. To do this requires that we change our thoughts of separation to one of unity and cooperation. There can be no real peace without it.

The simplest way to start is to understand your connection to all things and the divine energy that created you. Accept that the God you pray to is the same God we all pray to. There is no separate heaven for your religion. We all come from and return to the same place. No one needs to be converted. There is no wrong religion when it is founded on the principle of 'God is Love.' By removing this barrier of separation, we can all move forward with mutual respect for each other and our religions. We can all bask in the glory, joy, and love we receive when we live our life as God intended. That is our path to peace - The Nature of Being.

Part 2

Being the Light

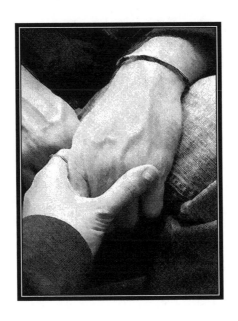

Chapter 11 - Discovering Your True Nature

Rebooting Your Beliefs

Discovering your true nature is a pivotal moment in life. Many people make this discovery at some point, forever changing the direction they're heading. The rest only find it in death.

You will understand and accept first, that your true nature is not of this flesh, and you are part of something far greater. Your Nature of Being is infinite, undying and unified with all things.

Secondly, you have everything you need to succeed and feel great joy already programmed in you from the start. This information was there at birth, but was quickly lost when your parents, family, friends and anyone you came in contact with, unknowingly fed you false information that they had been taught. This false sense of self has been recycled through the generations, causing the perception of our true nature to become skewed.

Most of my life I struggled with the belief that I needed to go out and leave my mark, and all the cruelty in the world was just part of the way things were and always will be. It was a strange feeling when I knew something didn't make sense, yet the information was coming from people I loved and trusted. It took a major event in my life like divorce to plunge me into a deep dive of soul searching that brought me where I am today.

I needed to understand the person I was becoming that led me to that low point in my life. Once I saw the misperceptions of my beliefs and began to move beyond my ego's influence, I was ready to perform the necessary work. With fresh eyes, I now see how easy it would have been to make this shift in consciousness without all the heartache and trauma.

One misguided idea some religions teach is that we will only be welcomed into heaven when we die - if we act a certain way and are faithful in life. To get into Club Heaven, we must follow the rules. We must be told what to do, and most importantly, we must have faith.

In essence we are told, "You will be judged, so forget what you know, and believe what you're told."

This perception externalizes the judgment of our actions to an outside source and gives us someone we need to answer to. What is the point of free will? When we surrender our freedom to choose to an organization or individual, we give up freedom altogether. We defer our responsibility to do what's right to the will of someone else. By removing our personal responsibility, we make it easy to justify war and murder as part of God's will.

It is important to remember that we are the one who is in control of our lives. Keep it simple. We are all part of God, so be like God, and live with love!

There's nothing to justify. There are no abstract philosophical answers to explain how faith works. You don't need to justify how the world that is only six-thousand years old. When we begin living with greater love and our faith centers on an infinite and unified existence, morality, compassion, and good choices follow.

I firmly believe life doesn't need to be hard, but to actualize a more fluid existence requires an understanding of our Nature of Being. It requires a journey that awakens the divine intuition inherent in all of us. My hope for you is that you begin to discover your true nature as soon as possible, and your children benefit from your wisdom from the day they are born, so they can pass it on to their children.

Introspectus

Your true nature is part of you. It has been with you since before you were born. It is the essence of your infinite self and was carried with you when you entered the physical world. It is the blue print for your Nature of Being. It's not the person you think you are or who your ego says you are. It is the person you are meant to become.

Think about your life for a moment. Think about all the influencers you've had, from your parents, spouse, family, friends, teachers, bullies and bosses. Why do you seek approval from these people in order to find context about who you are, when all this information is already within you?

Embrace your perfection. Uncover those dormant notions and ideas you instinctually know are true. Take time to look inward and unlock these parts of you. That is the secret to living a joyous, fulfilling, and balanced life. By doing so, you will no longer be looking for love; because you will come to realize that you are already the embodiment of love. Love naturally flows through you, originating from within and radiating outward. To attract love in your life, you need to be the love in your life. Call it self-love, but it's more than that. It's *absolute* love. It's *universal* love. I like to call it - *being*. You are being the person you naturally are. If you want to have faith, if you want to believe in something, believe in yourself.

As I've said before, all the answers are inside of you already. You will unlock them when you take the time to focus your attention inward. The process of doing this will become your *practice*. It will be part of your daily routine as much as brushing your teeth and combing your hair.

Begin by removing the things that do not serve your greatest good. For example, if you want to be more health conscious, you remove things that are unhealthy in your life. You adopt healthy eating habits and exercise more. If you want to find balance, peace of mind and live a more meaningful life, remove thoughts that don't serve you and adopt healthier ways of comprehending your reality and living your true nature.

Simplify your life. Simplify your thoughts and focus on what needs your attention the most. Be mindful and always in the moment.

Understanding old habits, not dwelling on the past, and adopting new ideas requires practice. Based on my experience, it's no easy feat. The wonderful thing is, it's an awakening! It's not a hardship. As you go through the process, it feels good, so you find you want to do it more. The only challenge is getting started.

Most of the resistance you'll feel in the beginning is your ego telling you can't. Every excuse you give for not taking the necessary steps is your ego convincing you that you're better off in your current state of suffering. When you let go of the fear and no longer believe that this is as good as it gets, the weight is lifted and you're free! You begin to remove the dead weight, clear out the clutter and focus on the thoughts that remain. You will find the one ideation originating from your true nature is - *I am love.*

As you take this journey, enjoy the ride. Remember, it's not a destination; it's a state of being. Timeless, in the moment, and always learning, the student becomes the teacher.

Your Practice

The journey to discover your true nature continues inward, getting you in touch with who you are, and why you do the things you do. You're going to want to make time for yourself, and this may be a drastic change for some of you, in this highly connected society we live in. To sit in quiet contemplation requires you to disconnect for a while.

This is your time - meditate. Listen to soft music or sit in silence with your thoughts. It's important to make meditation part of your routine for at least ten minutes each day. I've taken my practice on the road, exercising walking-meditation wherever I go. As I go about my busy-ness, I remain mindful and focused on the task, and quietly meditate throughout the day. I also enjoy taking long road trips, as the long drive allows me to sit quietly and organize my thoughts, clear out the clutter, and let it all go. Some of my best ideas have come to me on the road.

Yoga is another way to practice mindfulness and meditation, while getting a unique workout in as well. It combines stretching, balance and posture, with mindfulness and breathing. Someone once told me that they liked yoga but didn't buy into the "mystical" meditative aspect of it. I quickly concluded that they were not doing yoga, they were stretching. Yoga is the mental aspect of the exercise. It's a practice that allows you to instinctively quiet the mind, while being in the moment, focusing only on your physical movements and positions. It is a wonderful exercise in mindfulness.

Many enlightened people speak about the importance of meditation. Like yoga, it's a practice that originated in India and Asia, causing some people in the Western to have trouble relating to it. Yet, when they pray, they are already practicing meditation. Mediation is not difficult. It is not foreign. It will not magically transform you into a Buddhist.

Meditation is exercise for your mind. Not in the sense of solving puzzles and riddles or complex math equations, it's quite the opposite. It is the practice of focusing your mind on a single thought, removing the noise created by all the errant brainwork that clutters your mind at any given time. We need to give our minds a rest during waking hours, just as much as we need to rest our body when we sleep. And, if you've had a bad night's sleep, twenty minutes of meditation will make all the difference in the world.

I've found many great books and websites from the world's greatest teachers that offer valuable insight and experience to those who want to learn how to meditate. I've listed some of my favorites at the end of this book, and I encourage you to find other teachers who you can relate to and feels right to you.

Making meditation part of your practice comes down to just doing it. I began learning on my own. I started by relaxing in a chair, focusing on my breathing, and picking a single thought to give my attention to. Once I got that down, I began to expand by reading meditation books and listening to audio recordings.

Meditation is the gateway to understanding your inner-self and the energy centers in your body. It is a sacred time, and should be received as an ongoing gift from you. Accept that gift by integrating meditation into your daily routine. Develop a practice that focuses on both physical and mental wellness. Your physical wellbeing will only take you as far as your mental and spiritual wellbeing will allow. All the exercise in the world will not heal a broken spirit. Yet, a strong spirit at peace with itself makes the body stronger and more vital.

Chapter 12 – Qualities of Your True Nature

As you develop your practice, you will realize certain qualities you possess become more refined. These intrinsic virtues are in us all. Each is founded in love and is a component of love. Embrace them lovingly, as they reveal the person you are meant to be, and are becoming.

This chapter is not meant to be read straight through. Meditate on each quality as you read it. Look up their definitions for deeper context. Fully immerse yourself in each one for a day and begin to incorporate each quality into your process. As you define your Nature of Being through these daily meditations, build off of each one as it relates to experiencing greater love in your life. Pay special attention to how each one makes you feel, and how you can translate those feelings into your practice of *Being the Light*.

Honesty & Trust

When you're honest with yourself, you can be honest with others. There's no need for excuses or deception. You may not be perfect, but you're accountable. That's all you ever need to be. *What you see is what you get, so take me as I am.* This attitude allows me to feel safe in my own skin. I don't need to justify myself. I simply give an honest account of my actions, and do the best I can every day.

With honesty comes trust, one of the most valued virtues any two people can share. Without trust, we are alone. There is no society. As a collective society on Earth, honesty is coveted by all but never fully realized. Deep down we all want to trust each other. We need to trust each other for survival. The alternative to trust is the manipulation of trust through greed, selfishness, and other calling cards of the ego, and these human attributes have plagued or societies, cultures and governments from the beginning.

Honesty and trust on any scale begins within each individual, fostered in the roots of our own values. In order to know your "self" is to be honest with yourself. There is nowhere to hide from that one person who knows you best. Look deeply and without prejudice at all the aspects that you define as good and bad about you. How willing are you to illuminate the darkness within you? Without a complete understanding of what makes you tick, it's difficult to see that the only thing holding you back from being the amazing person you are meant to be is fear.

When you understand your own strengths and shortcomings, and stop catering to the shortcomings, you begin to face life more head on. You become more accountable for your actions, and excuses are no longer tolerated. Instead, you turn those shortcomings into the work you need to focus on in your practice. Don't use your strengths to compensate for your shortcomings. Use them to improve your whole self, the good and bad. You will advance when you combine an honest perception of yourself, accountability, and a willingness to improve.

As you begin to be more honest with yourself and make trust one of the primary virtues that people identify in you, mediate on the words *honesty* and *trust*. Look at all the ways you've been honest with yourself and with others. How does it make you feel? Then consider times when you may not have been so honest and how it makes you feel when you reflect on it. What feels better?

Imagine if you were honest 100% of the time with everyone, including yourself. How would this affect your beliefs and actions moving forward from here? Begin to identify with all the egocentric behaviors that prevent you from being honest all the time, and release them, as they are not part of your true nature. Let them go! Follow the path of what feels best, and remove the obstacles that are in the way of all the bliss that comes with your Nature of Being.

When you live your true nature, you can be honest to a fault. Honesty is never a bad thing. Nobody will ever fault you for it, as long as your honesty compels you to do the right thing. As you advance in your practice, remember that honesty is self-justifying. The more honest you are, and the more you can be trusted, the less you will need to ever prove that you're right.

So, when given a choice to be right or to be kind, always choose to be kind.

Kindness

Kindness is a direct result of love. You cannot be kind without love, and when you exist from a loving place, kindness is your nature. You can't help being kind to others. When you make others feel good, you feel good. Endorphins flow and you smile more.

Sharing and playing nice is one of the first lessons parents teach their children. Most children learn that in order to get what you want; they need to be willing to give. But, true kindness has no conditions or need for diplomacy. It's never forced or contrived. In its natural state, you never choose to be kind. You're just kind.

The best act of kindness is the one no one else knows about. To be boastful of your deed is self-serving, but nobody will ever judge you for it. Any act of kindness is a gift. A world of boastful kindness is still better than a world without kindness at all.

Kind acts need not be grandiose. A smile is sometimes all it takes. Saying "*Hello*" is of itself compassionate recognition of that person in your life. A smile honors their presence. My kids ask me why I say hello and start conversations with complete strangers in the grocery store checkout line. It's just who I am. It feels natural to me. I don't believe we're meant to be alone in this world, and the world needs more kindness. It's the little things that can make a difference in someone's life.

Kindness is extended through generosity. When we are kind, it's common to give, and when we give - all parties benefit. It's a mutual exchange of joy between people. Meditate on the idea of abundance through generosity and receiving by giving away. Nothing inspires me more than someone who can't afford to give yet does anyway, for they are blessed. Their abundance of spirit is greater than anything on Earth. Consider that all you have in this life is immaterial, and this fleeting expression of your infinite self does not define what or who you are. It is you who defines this experience.

As you begin each day, use the walking meditation exercise of mindfully maintaining only thoughts of love, and express those thoughts in kindness to whoever you meet. Then meditate on how this makes you feel, and follow your joy. What we all want more than ever is to feel good. Expressing love's virtues is the purest form of conscious bliss, as we create in concert with our creative source.

Caring & Compassion

I've heard it said that the opposite of love is hate, or fear. I believe the opposite of love is apathy, because it is expressionless. When you love, you care. To love someone is an outward expression of caring. To love yourself is to care about your own wellbeing. Any act of loving kindness is initiated by someone caring enough to take action to improve someone's life.

Empathy and compassion are two forms of caring. To have empathy is to understand and share the feelings of another.

To be compassionate is to walk in that person's shoes and feel their pain. Of the two, empathy inspires prayer and solidarity, compassion tends to invoke a willingness to take action. Having a deep sense of someone's pain, you channel the energy to heal through compassionate action.

The world would change for the better if more people would focus on greater compassion for the suffering of others. We all have the creative ability to contributor to solving problems, and it's everyone's responsibility to do just that. It's not enough to sit on the fence pointing fingers. True compassion comes with a willingness to do something about the suffering of others!

Meditate on compassion for at least five minutes every day. Consider what it feels like to suffer as others do, and pay attention to what drives you to be an idealist. Then take ownership of a cause, and affect changes that make this world a better place for everyone and everything. Let that cause to find you, and allow your passion to make it part of who you are. That is the essence of compassionate action.

Consider this: We live in a codependent world. We are here to help one another. We are the stewards of this planet and all its inhabitants. The promise of a better world rests on our ability to understand, support, and lift everyone up to their true potential. Open your eyes to the problems others are facing. Give your attention to solving those problems, and make compassionate action part of your Nature of Being.

Creativity & Inspiration

Creativity is born from inspiration. You are meant to do great things, and all your greatness lies in your ability to create.

Ask a child what he or she would rather do; homework, chores, or something creative like drawing or playing with clay. Children love to create and they are not so far removed from their creative source as some adults are. As folks get older, they may need to find inspiration to keep the creative process going. However, you rarely see a child going through a creative slump like writer's block.

Creativity is our most natural state of being. You are an extension of God's creative potential. The energy of the universe conspires in you to create as God creates. To be like God, create out of love, in the name of love and all that is good.

Inspiration is your connection with God and it comes in many subtle forms. Sometimes, you only need to listen. A friend recently told me he was thinking lovingly about his departed mother, when a bird landed next to him. He wondered if it was her, and I told him it must have been, because he willed it to be.

There are many amazing wonders we cannot even begin to understand. Miracles happen every day. I often find myself contemplating an answer, when a breeze blows across my face, telling me what I need to know. Animals appear at poignant moments, and people call me on the phone right when I think of them. These are not random acts.

When inspired, your natural-self creates freely. There are no blockages to processes, thoughts or emotions. Everything comes naturally, as if you're casually going along for the ride. It all feels good, and you create good emotion. That's the purpose for creating. You are meant to be happy. Creativity is the light that illuminates the darkness, diminishing negative emotions. Creativity comes from within, and there lies your happiness. As your natural self creates, your joy is awakened.

Meditate on what inspires you. As you do this, you will feel your passions well up inside. What are the emotions you feel and what are they focused on? It may be a project you've felt strongly about or something you've already started. Consider how you are involved in the creative process that feeds those passions. Let your mind go. Release any fear or doubt that makes you think you're not good enough or you don't have the means. Creativity is self-sustaining. Think of creativity in terms of limitless possibilities and allow for the details to be revealed. Inspiration will guide you through the process.

When love inspires greater love, your creative freedom is the greatest freedom of all.

Joy & Happiness

The search for happiness is a search for something that cannot be found outside of you. Joy and happiness are a state of being that exists when you are in alignment with your natural self. There is nothing to search for. You will experience happiness by allowing it into your life, by doing the things that bring you joy, benefit the world, and give you purpose.

At times, my happiness is stifled by circumstances beyond my control, creating insufferable stress. It's hard to be in a happy place when you get blindsided. I tend to lose momentum and stop creating. Then fear takes over. To quell this anxiety, it helps to remind myself that these problems need not define me and are only temporary. So, instead of reacting to negative emotions and dwelling in the problem, I'm able to remain in a constant state of love and joy, focusing only on what needs to be done. A problem will only be as big as you allow it to become, and by shifting your thoughts to a higher awareness, you free yourself to create again.

St. Francis of Assisi was affectionately known as the *Joyful Beggar*. He travelled the Italian countryside preaching his message of love with over a thousand people following him on his pilgrimage. With no means to feed them, his followers cried when there was no food to eat. Nonetheless, Francis assured them that if they had faith, all would be cared for. And when the situation looked most bleak, a caravan from a nearby village filled with townspeople wishing to express appreciation to Francis, arrived with food for everyone. Francis never lost faith, never left the path to his true nature, and always embodied the joy of God's love.

As you meditate on happiness, consider yourself a divine being whose real purpose is to love and be joyful. Joy results from living with greater love, and when you experience your Nature of Being and overflow with love's energy, joy radiates from you. Meditate on the idea that you are a love generating machine, and joy is what you're making. Think of all the ways you express joy, and be completely willing to give it away, so the world can feel its full effect.

Finally, pray more in times of joy, instead of praying when you need something. Divine inspiration is most accessible when you are experiencing high levels of grace, so take advantage of these elevated energy frequencies as they are happening. Recognize if your ego wants to show everyone how happy we are. Resist this temptation, as boasting only serves to squander your happiness. Instead, think of ways to channel your joy where it will do the most good.

Peace

Let there be peace on Earth. May peace be with you. Create a lasting peace. Peace among nations. Peace brother!

Where do you find peace? Like happiness, is it part of your true nature, or something that is either found or created? Questions like this have caused me to wonder if peace is a virtue of your Nature of Being or a byproduct of it. Peace can be a result of living your true nature. When all the qualities of my true self are functioning as one, I feel a deep sense of peace.

On one hand, to feel peaceful is to have little or no resistance working against you. Yet, do you really need to remove what's obstructing you to find peace, or does living peacefully help remove it for you? Consider the first option. If finding peace becomes an exercise to remove resistance, this requires work. To find peace within, all the virtues of your Nature of Being must first be in alignment. Peace among nations requires the rigors of conflict and negotiation before any peace can be made. This approach may be putting the cart before the horse.

In preparing to write this section, I began meditating on the meaning of peace. Coincidentally, I did this when I had a good deal of stress on my mind. As I closed my eyes and visualized the word peace and what it means to me, something magical happened. My stress almost instantly subsided. My troubles didn't go away, but I was able to let them go of it. It was as if I took a broom and swept them off to the side to make way for this wonderful feeling. I found that by just meditating on the word, I was able to feel more peaceful, allowing for sustained feelings of joy and contentment.

In a roundabout way, this exercise taught me that peace brings about peace. By being peaceful, you bring peace into your life. If you want peace on Earth or peace among nations, be peaceful! Peace is not found in conflict or finagled negotiations. It is born from a willingness to let go and live the joy and contentment that peace brings. If it is a byproduct of anything, it is a byproduct of hope. For this reason alone, peace is most surely a virtue of your Nature of Being!

Try this exercise for yourself. Meditate on the word peace and contemplate its meaning. Think of it as already part of you, a common characteristic of your being. There is no level of trying to be peaceful. Allow peace to become you. Perform this meditation when you're feeling stressed, and see if it helps to bring any seemingly big problems into a more meaningful perspective.

Also, always be peaceful when dealing with others. Allow all the faculties of your true nature come into play, and remember that peace is not for you alone. It is an intention of love that is meant for all. There is no inner peace without expressing peace to others.

Abundance

Abundance is a state of mind. Consider two people of identical means. One feels abundant. The other feels poor. It's a matter of perception.

What does abundance mean?

- Is it having lots of stuff?
- Do you feel abundant with the things you already have?
- Would you feel abundant if you had less?
- Would you feel abundant if it was all gone?

It's hard to pinpoint why some of the happiest nations in the world are also the poorest ones financially. Yet countries like Bhutan in southern Asia have begun to put the nation's happiness ahead of gross national product, adding a Ministry of Happiness to their government and adopting a happiness quotient to measure the country's gross national happiness. It's logical. When happiness and creativity are in alignment together, people feel more happy, creative, and productive.

Those who believe abundance comes through the accumulation of material goods get frightened when they hear how enlightened people often give up their worldly possessions. Yet, nothing could be further from the truth. To be enlightened, you don't need to give up anything unless you really want to. What these people fail to see is that you don't need possessions to feel peace or joy. Abundance comes through contentment. No one will ever tell you to give up the finer things in life, but as wisdom gives you clearer vision; you may begin to see frivolous opulence as unnecessary.

What once brought you happiness loses its attraction when you realize happiness is already within you.

Have you ever seen a young child open a gift, and be more interested in the box the present was in? Sometimes it's the little things that bring us the greatest joy. Redefine what it is to be content, appreciating the things you have. You will begin to simplify your life quite effortlessly, once you discover there's greater stress in getting what you want as opposed to being content with what you got.

I've learned to be more observant of everything around me. This allows me to appreciate life more. Consequently, I've become a better listener, enjoying much deeper, fulfilling relationships as a result. This practice has opened a whole new level of abundance in my life. Humans are a social species. We're all meant to interact and enhance each other's lives. Every person you meet is an opportunity to give and receive all the gifts that life has to offer. The core of this abundance is *love*.

Love's ability to bring about joy and contentment is uncomplicated. All the qualities that define your natural self coalesce. Caring, compassion, honesty, kindness, joy, creativity, connectedness, peace, and gratitude all manifest through love to bring abundance to life. It's a part of the karmic reaction caused by living with greater love, and doing the things God intended you to be when you were born. That is the secret to living an abundant life.

Begin the practice of experiencing love at every moment. Meditate on love and carry that feeling with you through your day. Center your thoughts on love at every moment, expressing yourself to others with silent blessings. Experiencing this intention is the purest form of giving and receiving abundance.

Use love as the cornerstone for all you do. A foundation built on love is not easily crumbled. Live your passion as if you've already arrived, visualizing your success, and then follow through as you put all the pieces into place.

Gratitude

I reflect on my life and the gifts I've been given, feeling a profound sense of gratitude. I know I'm an infinite being, yet here I am in physical form, living and breathing along side of you, sharing experiences, and being the loving intention I know I'm meant to be.

I'm most grateful to know love, and be able to express the joy, creativity, kindness, and compassion of my true nature. I've been gifted with rational thought. This allows me to comprehend the truth of my existence. It's freed me from the turmoil of my humanness that caused me to separate from my Nature of Being in the past. This gratitude now fills me with even greater love. Love and gratitude are reciprocative by nature. The more I love, the more grateful I am. The more grateful I am, the more I love!

I find gratitude in everything I touch. All experiences, good or bad, have brought me to where I am today. Every experience is a lesson. Every lesson brings me closer to my true self, inspires me to grow, and reminds me of my infinite nature. When I'm walking my intended path, I'm awestruck! I cannot help feeling grateful.

Gratitude is one of the most essential interactions between people, and fills a fundamental need to feel appreciated. It's inspired by an expression of love. *Thank you* is synonymous with *I love you*, and is an affirmation of appreciation, honoring another person's selflessness.

Think of love as energy in motion, in a constant state of attraction. Your love is actualized and appropriated to wherever you choose to send it. Acts of kindness and expressions of gratitude are the exchange mechanisms for love's flow. When you feel gratitude, you are fully engaged with that energy exchange.

As you meditate on gratitude, think of all you've been given, starting with the good. Think of the gift of life and the opportunity it has afforded you. Think of all the people who have entered your life and made it better. Without going down memory lane, focus on the love you feel as you envision them in your mind. Consider the material things in your life, the home that gives you shelter, the food that sustains you, and any creature comforts. If you've been abundantly blessed, contemplate how it feels to have the means to give freely to others. Allow love and gratitude to fill your contentment, and say a silent prayer of gratitude.

Any experience you consider to be bad also deserves your appreciation. Don't dwell on the past. Instead, look at all events collectively as learning lessons that give you wisdom, strength and fortitude. Use gratitude as a mechanism for turning any negative event into something positive. Say a prayer for the bumps, bruises, and scars you've earned while you were figuring your life out. Be grateful you survived and learned from it. Turn that gratitude into self-love and conviction, so you can move forward from here, and exist from the highest plain of your true nature.

Love, Faith and the Prayer of St. Francis

I conclude this chapter by offering the best gift of my Catholic upbringing. You don't need to be Catholic or Christian to appreciate the Prayer of St. Francis of Assisi. It is one of the world's most perfect prayers, and has always ' ~~n very dear to me. I say it often and contemplate its ~ me define who I am.

The Prayer of St. Francis of Assisi

Heavenly Father make me an instrument of your peace.
Where there is hatred let me sow love.
Where there is injury, pardon
Where there is doubt, faith
Where there is despair, hope
Where there is darkness, light
And where there is sadness, joy

God grant that I not so much seek to be consoled as to console,
to be understood as to understand,
to be loved as to love.
For it is in the giving that we receive.
It is in the pardoning that we are pardoned.
And it is in the dying we are born to eternal life.

I encourage you to meditate on this prayer. Feel its joy, and consider the following thoughts:

- Have faith in yourself, because you have God's love within you. You will need this faith if you are to have faith in others. Having faith in your own perfection will guide you in being free of any conflict within yourself.

- You cannot control other's thoughts and actions, but you can free yourself of guilt, and reduce your own conflict within. Seeking to do the right thing sets you apart from all others who are doing their own thing. Once you become an instrument of peace, you will stand up and stand out. You will be the way for others to follow and realize their own divine light.

- Your faith in others reaches new heights, because you now see perfection in all people. Your ego will quickly warn you that your blind faith leaves you vulnerable to attack. People will take advantage of you. We've created this false existence, where everyone has trust issues. Yet, giving of yourself allows people to recognize and appreciate your worthiness to receive their love. It is the only way you will genuinely receive their faith and be loved in return.

- It is in the giving that we receive, so give freely without expectations of getting anything back. In doing so, you satisfy yourself, because your love is self-sustaining. Remember that it is human nature to be love. Love is never lost! For every one person who lets you down, there are hundreds, maybe thousands of people who want exactly what you want and would be glad to give love to you in return.

- It is in the pardoning that we are pardoned, so forgive those who do not return your love, for they know not what they are doing. Forgiveness is the ultimate teaching tool. Having faith in the power of unconditional love within you allows you to teach others that it is okay to let go and be love. They may not learn the lesson right away, but your experience in their life will always leave an impact. In time, they will learn.

- Also remember to be forgiving of yourself. When you return to your Nature of Being, there is no need to carry the burdens of your past once the lessons have been learned.

- It is in dying we are born to eternal light. If you never know God's love in life, you will know it in death, but you do not need to die to know its power. Once you let go of ego's grip, you will know the absolute, perfect and eternal love that is in all of us. To know this, is to learn life's ultimate lesson while you're still living.

Chapter 13 - The Four Cardinal Virtues

Five-hundred years before the birth of Jesus, Chinese philosopher Loa Tzu wrote the eighty-one verses of the Tao Te Ching. His teachings were the foundation of Taoism, and the Tao Te Ching is a guide for many today living a more spiritual, enlightened life. Lao Tzu also taught what he called the *Four Cardinal Virtues*. When applied to my perception of the world, these tenets for living a more balanced life help keep me centered on my path, living in greater peace. Be mindful of the Four Cardinal Virtues, incorporating them into your daily routine, as they can be very helpful to jumpstart your practice.

#1: Reverence for All Living Things

I have a friend who is an avid hunter. Each autumn he goes deer hunting so his family will have venison to live off of through the year. Though he could easily go to the supermarket to buy his meat, he believes it's important to know where his food comes from.

When I was first introduced to his tradition, I stood looking at the deer he'd shot, as it lay in his yard waiting to be processed. I noticed that in the mouth of the deer was a sprig of evergreen leaves. Naively, I joked that he shot the buck while it was eating. My friend quickly corrected me, explaining that he had placed the leaves in its mouth after the animal was dead, as part of a traditional German prayer in reverence and gratitude for the animal giving its life to feed his family.

To have reverence for all living things is to understand oneness. We are all part of the Earth's global ecosystem, performing our part in the ebb and flow of life and death, just as any other creature on the planet does. Each species fits perfectly in its place, and all plants and animals serve a purpose. Species evolve, while others go extinct. This is the natural order of life, and we humans play a pivotal role in this process. It's essential that we have respect for *all things*, including the planet itself.

We are one species out of millions that has the ability to understand the impact we have and choose how we make that impact felt. We knowingly affect and manipulate the so many living things on a daily basis, for better or for worse.

When there is reverence for all life, responsible choices are instinctively made. There is a natural sense of appreciation and compassion that is devoid of cruelty. Many people adjust their diets and buying habits based on these feelings.

Some are less inclined to stomp on a bug for no reason. When there is reverence for life, we begin to see the world with a new set of eyes. We grasp the connectedness of all things. Our vision expands beyond our field of view to include the world as a whole, comprehending how everything functions in ever-changing synchronicity.

Finding balance is not to arrive at a condition where everything stays the same. Balance is found when we function within the changing flow of all life. The planet itself is alive and breathing, and will go on long after you and I are gone. We must learn to live within this flow and that begin to appreciate and understand what that means.

It's also important to note that we cannot have reverence for all life without adopting a similar attitude towards other people as well. We cannot help this planet without wanting to help each other. Life is a struggle for survival; regardless of wealth, religion, or politics. I don't expect everyone to agree. However, how we choose to survive and how we affect those around us can make all the difference.

When there is reverence for life, there is respect. When there is reverence for life, there is greater love, compassion and empathy. When there is reverence for life, we are consciously thinking globally and making decisions based on what's best for all people. The important thing to remember is we don't have to always agree. We just need to make choices based on what's right. Decisions based on love, originating from our natural-selves, are always the right decisions.

When I meditate on this virtue, I no longer feel separate from other life. I'm mindful of ego's need to convince me that I'm somehow different, yet I find that you can avoid falling into this trap by being aware of my connectedness and respecting all living things, no matter how small, ugly, or icky you've originally perceived them to be.

Meditate on the perfection of it all, understanding how species are perfectly adapted for their environment. They all serve a role in the wellbeing of this planet. There are no accidents. Each creature, every plant, bug, fish, bird and person is here for a reason. All life is precious. We understand its meaning through knowledge, compassion, and respect.

Seeing the Wonder of it All

Begin to observe the world in greater detail. Pay close attention to the littlest things, and take time to notice their wonders. Walk outside, and take account of all the living things around you. Even in urban areas, life abounds. I'm always amazed how animals like pigeons and squirrels have adapted to living in big cities, how falcons and hawks nest atop tall buildings, and plants have the ability to push their way through solid concrete in search of sunlight.

In spite of the resilience of some creatures, life on Earth can be quite fragile. Imagine a world without bees and other pollinating insects for instance. Their absence would make this a very different place. Think of the Earth as a living, breathing entity. We cling to it like a baby clings to its mother. Allow this level of empathy to strengthen your sense of connection.

Begin to observe all people and learn to appreciate our diversity. We've been blessed with a countless number of amazing individuals, all different, and all trying to find their way. Imagine a world where more people got along, where there was mutual respect, and reverence for life. What would that be like? Imagine the possibilities! Imagine it as if it was already here, and make the effort to do the impossible. Simply open your heart and let it in.

Embrace your connection to all living things, and you'll take a huge leap into understanding your divine nature. Without feeling separate from it, you will find yourself completely immersed in the spirit of creation, knowing you are part of something far greater than yourself.

#2: Natural Sincerity

When you meet someone for the first time, what are the first thoughts that come to mind? Are you noticing certain things about them? Are you sizing them up? Are you trying to gauge if this person can help you - or hurt you? Do you see the divine spirit within them that connects the two of you together with the rest of the universe?

When you meet an old friend, a family member or someone from your past, what are the first thoughts that come to mind? Are you sizing them up? Are you remembering past memories? Loving memories? Are you thinking about the money they owe you or how they hurt you? Or do you see the divine spirit within them that connects the two of you with the rest of the universe?

When you people watch in a crowd, do you judge others by the way they look or the color of their skin? Are you annoyed because they're in your way? Do you randomly judge them without knowing anything about them? Or do you see the divine spirit within them that connects the two of you with the rest of the universe?

The way we perceive others is often defined by how we perceive ourselves. Our feelings and attitudes towards others often mirror what we feel privately. When we are judgmental toward others, we are being our own worst critic. When we condemn others, we condemn ourselves. Conversely, when we see the divine light in others, we see the divine light in ourselves. Our attitude towards others reflects both the good and bad we see in ourselves, so choose to focus on what serves you best.

Natural sincerity comes when you are conscious of your divine light. It's a consequence of having respect, being free of judgment, and acting upon your divinity. It manifests when your true-self is leading with love.

The virtue of natural sincerity places you squarely grounded in your Nature of Being. The mask is off, and people can see you exactly for who you are. For some, this vulnerability may seem unnerving. We tend to go through life wearing various masks that show people only what we want to show them. That is the persona of the ego, always feeling the need to protect you. In all reality, when you are being insincere and wearing one of your other masks, there's a good chance people can see right through you anyway. As the saying goes; you can fool some of the people some of the time, but you can't fool all the people all the time. So, why bother?

Find strength in vulnerability. Love can do no harm. You have nothing to hide, so there's no need to feel vulnerable. You can accept the perfection of being imperfect. You are free to express yourself with sincerity, without any need to worry about what others think. People won't run from you, or avoid you. Quite the opposite, you will find people are more attracted to you. They trust you more. Your friendships are stronger because of that trust.

Wearing the Face of Sincerity

Make an effort to embrace this virtue by allowing sincerity to be the only face people see. Pay close attention to your thoughts, being totally honest with others and yourself. Make it a conscious effort to be in alignment with the face of sincerity. Never put anyone down, and never place yourself above others. Instead, be humble and see others for the gift they bring to the world. Be of service to them, and always think of what you can do to elevate them, instead of what you can gain from them.

See yourself as a loving, divine spirit who is connected to all things. Strengthen your own self image by embracing your divine connection. When you are stronger on the inside, there is no need for any masks. Everything about you that anyone needs to know is open for all to see.

#3: Gentleness

In my youth, I was a bit of a showboat. I wore loud clothes. I was outspoken. I purposely stood out and wanted everyone to take notice of me. I was opinionated, and did far more talking than listening. I remember thinking that by age twenty-five; I would know everything I needed to know. I actually set a goal for myself, and by my twenty-fifth birthday, I pretty much knew everything I wanted to know at the time. It's funny because since then, I've needed to reevaluate and relearn much of what I thought was true.

I've mellowed quite a bit too. I tend to keep my opinions to myself, and I've surrendered my need to be right all the time. I do far more listening now than talking. I'm more open to new ideas. And, to the delight and well being of those nearest to me, I stopped dressing so loudly. Over the years, quiet wisdom took over where bravado once covered up for my naiveté and lack of experience.

When I entered adulthood, the intended path seems straight at first. The wide open road seems just right for putting the pedal to the metal and picking up speed. However, it was only a matter of time before I realized the road is full of hills and valleys, twists and turns. I discovered that needed to throttle back before I flew out of control.

The virtue of gentleness has many facets. There is greater intention towards mild, deliberate action, and less towards abrupt reaction. It is synonymous with kindness and tenderness, and requires a person to be adept in sensitivity. The tough guy must also be a loving father. Gentleness allows you to be vulnerable, accepting your own fragility, and surrendering ego's boastful bravado. There's less need to prove that you're something other than your true nature's desire to just "be."

All stress is self-imposed. How often do you beat yourself up over circumstances that don't go your way? Learn to be gentle with yourself. I once had bipolar tendencies. I would ride high on emotions when times were good and land hard when things went wrong. When I finally understood that nothing lasts forever and life is an ever-changing series of highs and lows, I found that it was best to remain somewhere in the middle.

Gentleness allows you to be more pliable and able to adapt to changing situations. As water flows gently, it always finds the easiest path, adjusting its course as it encounters obstacles. Like water, you too are constantly moving and changing. Exercise enduring patience. Have the flexibility and finesse to make life's ups and downs smoother and softer, remaining more balanced with your feelings. Being free of emotional extremes helps you make better decisions.

When you encounter resistance in life, it's rarely advantageous to force an outcome. Like trying to loosen a screw that's stuck, you risk stripping the threads if you muscle it too hard. Sometimes, the best strategy is to step back and evaluate the situation, to understand it better and find alternative solutions. Gentleness constrains impulsive behavior and allows you to exercise careful caution when making decisions.

Adopting a Gentle Nature

Bring greater gentleness to your life by giving attention to your movements and thoughts. Are you graceful, or are your actions abrupt and awkward? Work on refining the motions of your daily routines. The attention you give to your movements focuses your mind to be more graceful. It also does wonders for your golf swing. Slowing down emotional impulses will result in more deliberate thoughts. You might just find life less chaotic and more peaceful because of it.

Slow down and adopt the pace of nature. The oak tree spends the first part of its life quietly growing its roots deep and building a firm trunk, before it begins to reach for the sky. Always take the time to do your best work.

If you give a group of young children an art project, some of them might cut out a bunch of shapes and meticulously glue them to the paper. There is order and purpose to the shapes, sizes and the colors they use. Other children will quickly cut large, random shapes, glue them down, and only seem interested in getting it done. Give the same project to a group of adults and most of them will take their time creating a masterpiece, because they've learned to slow down and appreciate the process. For many, gentleness is a virtue that is learned over time.

Finally, allow gentleness to be the essence of your expression of love to others. It's alright to expose your vulnerabilities, and allow love to be articulated with absolute sincerity. There is natural gentleness to it. Even the toughest manly-man will softly say "I love you" to his wife or child, and be unable to control his voice as it goes up an octave. That is the gentleness that love brings.

#4: Supportiveness

A thread by itself is weak and easily broken. Many threads together form a chord, and you now have a strong rope. It's obvious that we are all stronger together. We all face difficulties in life, and there is no feeling more fearful than the isolation and loneliness of facing those difficulties on our own. Sometimes, we need a shoulder to cry on. Sometimes, we need someone who can offer a new point of view, a fresh perspective, or someone who can talk us down from the edge of despair. Supportiveness offers a safety net for all.

The goal of supportiveness is to raise each person up to their true potential, to be strong enough to stand on their own. In turn, we can then work together to assist the next one in need. That is the essence of community.

The cornerstone of supportiveness is family. I was fortunate enough to grow up the youngest of seven siblings. At times we fought like cats and dogs, but there was never a time I felt unloved or unsupported. As we grew up, our bond became unshakeable.

Not everybody can be as fortunate as I. There are families who've not talked to each other in years, parents who no longer communicate with their children, family members who are shunned because they are gay. These are the unfortunate effects of misaligned belief and prejudices. The maternal, paternal and fraternal bonds of family are the strongest, most essential bonds we can have. Without this foundation family, the entire system of community breaks down.

As a global society, we need to grow up and realize no matter how much we argue or disagree, in the end we're all family. The Earth is our home, and we all live under the same roof. We're not going to get along all the time, but if we maintain the undercurrent of love as we have with our blood relatives, we will grow and mature as siblings do.

The solution to most of the world's societal problems rests in our ability to recognize all people, regardless of race, creed, country or sexual preference as our brothers and sisters.

If you look at nature, supportiveness is the chord that holds all things together. There is give and take among all things. Animals depend on each other for survival. They depend on vegetation for food. The plants provide life sustaining oxygen, while the animals return carbon dioxide to the plants. We all work in symbiosis. Water is the essence of life, and even water relies on hydrogen and oxygen for its existence. When we die, our physical forms are returned to the Earth and nothing is wasted. Our planet is one great support system for all life.

Being Supportive and Giving Back

As you contemplate Lao Tzu's Fourth Cardinal Virtue, consider your place among all things. Breathe in the air that sustains you, and remember that it came from the tree outside your window. Next time you take a drink of water, consider that the liquid in your glass once flowed in the currents of an ocean and fell as rain half way around the globe. The oxygen that helps create the H_2O of that water was once inhaled by your ancestors, exhaled and then absorbed by a tree in the Amazon Rainforest.

As the cycle of life continues, here you are; a living breathing part of it. While you're here, take from it freely. Drink a glass of water, breathe the air, but always remember that at some point, you will give back. That is the natural order of things.

Make it a point to wake up every day and ask, "How may I be of service?" Allow your greatness to define you by giving and being supportive of others. Make amends with estranged family and friends. Reach out and begin repairing bridges that have caused any disconnect in your life. Extend yourself to strangers. Offer a smile and assistance when it's needed. The solution to any global problem begins with individual effort. The threads of life become stronger the more we work together. So let it be done.

Countless Virtues

In closing this chapter, I'm giving you an exercise. Go back and review the previous chapter. List all the qualities of your natural self that I defined. Combine them with Lao Tzu's Four Cardinal Virtues, and then create your own list of qualities and virtues that define love, and what it means to live with greater love. Contemplate them all through meditation. Consider ways to apply them into your daily life, and allow them become part of your practice.

The more you learn and spend time thinking about living God's intention, the closer you come to being God-realized and living your Nature of Being.

I also encourage you to create conversations with friends and family, especially your children. The more you talk about love and keep it in the forefront of your mind, the more you make it part of your daily life. In doing so, you fulfill the dharma bestowed on us all - the role of the teacher. We are charged with teaching others about our Nature of Being, the light inside all of us, and our need to shine brightly.

The Four Cardinal Virtues:

1. Reverence for All Living Things
2. Natural Sincerity
3. Gentleness
4. Supportiveness

Other Virtues:

_____

_____

_____

_____

_____

_____

_____

_____

Chapter 14 - Be the Light

Time to Shine

There is a touch of irony that I'm writing this final chapter in the aftermath of the Orlando Nightclub Massacre, the deadliest mass shooting in the United States to date. I conceived this book just prior to the Charlie Hebdo shootings in Paris. Within the time of writing this book there's been a seemingly endless number of bombings, murders and acts of terror. I have never felt more strongly about my need to write this book.

One day the world will wake up and realize that the status quo is not working. The problems of the world are so deeply ingrained in history and politics, that a wholesale resetting of how we are conducting ourselves seems inevitable. My biggest concern is how many more people need to die? How much more suffering do we need to endure before things improve for all and not just a select few?

Love is the answer. My thanks go to John Lennon for instilling those words in me. More songs need to be written about love's true nature. More movies and books need to be written, before the sleeping world wakes up. I'm always optimistic that love will prevail because I know that in time, light will illuminate the darkness. It's our destiny as human beings to achieve enlightenment, to be God-realized and God-actualized.

Looking down the path, it seems like a long road we all must travel. The question is, how long will you sit at the starting line before you choose to begin this journey? Together we can change the world, but it's going to take enough people to reach critical mass before we achieve any real change. So, what are you waiting for? Your time has come. Be the light, and shine brightly.

Through Your Hands

You can dream of a better world, or you can do something about it. Each one of us is given divine gifts that allow us to make a difference in this world. What you choose to do with those gifts defines your greatness. Greatness is in you. You don't need to win a Nobel Prize, a Super Bowl Ring or an Academy Award. Greatness is defined by how you use your talents throughout your life and to what degree you leave this world a better place. That is lasting greatness.

The late great Walter Payton was one of the most prolific running backs in football history, shattering nearly every running record in football, yet he will likely be remembered most for his kindness, charity and good nature he brought to others. He was the incarnation of love. Having the skills of being a famous football player propelled him into the limelight for that love to shine.

When your life is done, make it a point to leave this world better because you were here. It doesn't matter what you do for a living. No matter how famous you are, your actions will be remembered by those you've touched and will live forever through them.

If your life doesn't suit you, change it. Do what you love, and do it with love. If you want to be a ditch digger, be the best darn ditch digger there ever was - and do it with love. When you live life with joy, you won't be judged for the job you do or the amount of wealth you acquire.

If you have a great idea resting dormant, you must fulfill it. Don't let your greatness die within you. If the world will be a better place because of it, then it is your obligation to pursue that dream and live the life you were meant to live.

Most importantly, do what feels right. I've been accused of being a dreamer. Who am I to think I can write a book about change? Yet, I've been put here for this reason. My only failure would be to never start writing. I encourage you to dream big and swing for the fences. But most importantly, you got to take a swing. You can't let the pitches go by and expect to walk the bases.

When you're in alignment with your natural self and focused on doing the right thing, mighty power will come to your aid. You'll find strength and resources you never knew you had. The right people will show up at just the right time, and the right choices will be made. The world needs you! There are lots of problems to be solved, yet nothing that can't be fixed. It just takes thought and effort.

Indeed, the world needs you right now. Don't squander the opportunity to do what you are destined to become. Your divine purpose is to "be" love. Love in all its form and motion creates the synchronicity that allows there to be harmony in the universe. This harmony is dependent upon all the musicians to be on the same note at the same time. It will take everyone to play their part.

The Simple Things

Sometimes it's the simplest things in life that make all the difference. These are also the things that are most often overlooked. The power of *Please, Thank You, God Bless You,*

Shalom, Namaste, and even a simple *Hello* can have more of an impact than the grandest gestures of kindness. Their cumulative effect fuels the engines of love, compassion and kindness. Every gesture is recognition of another person's presence in your life. You honor their presence and the divine unity you share.

These simple blessings create ripples of kindness. Ripples create waves, and pretty soon there is motion. This motion creates shifts in perception. One act of kindness inspires another. The more people give, the more lives are touched by kindness and soon, the light of kindness begins to shine brightly.

The essence of love is a simple recognition of our divine connection to one another. Next time you see someone, greet them with a smile. Remember that every greeting, thank you, and acknowledgment of another person's divine grace in your life is an expression of love. You acknowledge their gift to the world, and what a great gift that is.

So I say to you:

What a great gift you are in my life. Thank you for your presence here. Thank you for the simple kindness you bring with your smile. Thank you for your conscious effort to make this world a better place. Thank you for the love you give each day. Because of you, I am truly blessed!

Love Does Not Require Sacrifice

To love is to be in a natural state of giving, and does not require sacrifice. It's misleading to believe that to sacrifice; you are giving up something in anticipation of gaining salvation in return. This implies you're giving of yourself in exchange for something you already have. You already are an infinite, loving soul, and true giving has no expectations of reward. Love offers nothing other than to experience love. Therefore, it is senseless to sacrifice in order to receive salvation, when it's already part you. You only need to surrender your ego, be the embodiment of love, and experience the true essence of your natural self.

Sacrifice can be a condition of guilt. When we sacrifice out of guilt, we are not at peace with ourselves. Only through love can we atone for our sins. To experience peace and free ourselves of guilt, we only need to love. When there is love, we give things freely and hold no attachments to them, expecting nothing in return.

To grasp this fully is to understand the essence of your being. If I die saving someone's life, my life is given freely for another. There is no sacrifice, only my gift to the one I saved. I'm not afraid to die, because I'll never truly die. My body would be gone, but I am eternal. This notion is instrumental in letting go of ego. Let go of your physical existence and stop thinking of yourself as John Smith or Susan Somebody. That's just a name given to you at birth. Instead, think of yourself in terms of; *I am God incarnate, I am love, I am one,* because that's who you really are.

Inspiring Greater Love

Inspiring greater love is to actively encourage others to feel love more and express love more, through the love you give showing them the way. They in turn will do like you, creating growing cycles of loving intention that gets passed on to more and more people. There's an endless supply of love inside us all. It's self-generating and has the ability to grow exponentially by all who are touched by it.

Inspired acts of kindness bring about this chain reaction. Kindness elevates a person's happiness, making it easier for them to let go and be inspired. When someone feels the euphoria of receiving, it's hard not want to give as well. So, give gifts of all sizes, big and small, whenever possible. Kindness is a gift of love, the most elementary form of inspiration.

When you encounter either a loved one or a so-called enemy, the connection is always the same. Differences matter little when your goal is to inspire greater love. Love is never ambivalent. It never chooses sides. Love only promotes goodness. When you are faced with a challenging relationship, one of the greatest tools you have is your ability to understand the other person's plight. Having compassion and focusing it outwardly in an effort to ease their pain is to exercise the true mastery of love.

It seems paradoxical to love your enemies, but love will reveal the way things really are. To love your enemy is to understand fully them. By removing the darkness surrounding them, you begin to see with greater clarity. You will find they are not your enemy at all, and you have more in common than you realize. Like you, they have brothers and sisters and friends. They have a soul that is intrinsically connected to you and to God. They are someone with their own set of needs who perhaps like you, just needs to be shown the light.

We may not all share the same values. We may have cultural differences. We may have different religious ideals, but when we are inspired by greater love, we lose our judgments and see only commonalities. If we let go of all misconceptions that breed hatred and focus on what makes us the same and not what makes us different, we may find the term enemy really doesn't exist at all.

Knowledge and understanding are your greatest assets. Hatred is blind. Open your heart and your mind before you cast any judgment. Avoid living in a bubble that blinds you to the needs of others. Take action to ease their pain. Let your kindness be an example of your loving awareness, and you will take great strides to inspire love in both your life and in those you touch.

Do it with joy. Actively seek to lift people up with your love, and inspire them. Be the person who lights up the room when you enter. Tell people about something amazing you saw today. Compliment them, and let your natural sincerity show. Allow the focus of conversation to be on them and not on you, with the goal of making them smile.

Your love will free those you touch from their sorrow and negative emotions. When you bring joy, kindness and understanding to another person's life, you help to release them from the conditions that are limiting their own love to flow. When you inspire greater love, encourage this feeling of freedom. Elevate their spirit to fly free.

Love is something that we all need and desire. It's a limiting belief that love is outside us and needs to be searched for and found. In truth, love is a divine gift, the essence of our being, and comes in an endless supply. There is no greater gift or aspiration than to inspire others to realize their own greater sense of love. We do it by example, by being the love we want in our own lives, and giving it freely with kindness, joy and understanding.

Leading with Love

I see two ways we can reach a Golden Age, and we will get there one way or the other. If we follow our current path and destroy the planet or each other, those who are left will understand. They will finally learn from our mistakes and rebuild with humility from the lessons learned. The other alternative is that we all become God realized and begin a new era of God actualization. This will require a paradigm shift in consciousness, from a world in fear to a world in love.

The world needs leaders, so why not begin with you? Embrace your Nature of Being. Take the high road. Adopt a habit of giving, and allow compassion and creativity to guide your thoughts and actions. Build a culture that is based on cooperation and less on competition. Be the teacher, and the beacon for others to follow.

Let it begin with you. Allow your awareness of your natural state of being to become the source of your inspiration, motivation and love. Let your creativity be your outward expression of that love. Be the change you want to see in the world, and live it every day. Take the love challenge and begin to alter your thoughts to be in alignment with your loving natural self. Let go of old, outmoded beliefs that restrict you, and trust in the change you are becoming.

This is not a religious movement. It is a shift in consciousness. It is an awakening that allows you to discover your true nature and become the person you were meant to be. I speak from experience, because it has changed my life. It will change your life too. Lose your fear and let love guide you.

Love always. Always love!

Credits

The author would like to acknowledge all who have contributed material & assisted in the writing of this book.

The Nature of Being was made possible by the following:

All quotes from *A Course in Miracles* © are from the Third Edition, published in 2007. They are used with permission from the copyright holder and publisher, the Foundation for Inner Peace, P.O. Box 598, Mill Valley, CA 94942-0598, www.acim.org and info@acim.org.

Material Also Inspired by:

Dass, Ram & Das, Rameshwar *Be Love Now: The Path of the Heart*, New York, HarperOne 2010 ISBN: 9780061961373

Dyer, Wayne *Inspiration*, New York: Hay House, 2007 ISBN: 9781401907228

Dyer, Wayne *The Power of Intention*, New York: Hay House, 2005 ISBN: 9781401902162

Jung, Carl *Modern Man in Search of a Soul.* London: Trubner and Co., ISBN: 1933 0-15-661206-2 (Mariner Books edition)

Millman, Dan *Way of the Peaceful Warrior*, Novato, CA, New World Library 2000 ISBN: 0915811898

Nhat Hanh, Thich *Thich Nhat Hanh: Essential Writings*, Maryknoll, NY, Orbis Books 2001 ISBN: 1-57075-370-9

Nhat Hanh, Thich *The Miracle of Mindfulness*, Boston, Beacon Press 1975 ISBN: 978-0-8070-1239-0

Selby, John *Kundalini Awakening*, New York: Bantam Books, 1992 ISBN: 0-553-35330-6

Professional Services:

Manuscript Consultant: Terry Pfister *Professional Writer*, Marketing & Communications

Concept Consultation and Inspiration: Mary Jane Pfister

Made in the USA
Middletown, DE
29 February 2020